Empath

Your Guide to Understanding Empaths and Their Emotional Abilities to Feel Empathy, Including Tips for Highly Sensitive People, Dealing with Energy Vampires, and Being a Psychic Empath

© **Copyright 2018**

All Rights Reserved. No part of this book may be reproduced in any form without permission in writing from the author. Reviewers may quote brief passages in reviews.

Disclaimer: No part of this publication may be reproduced or transmitted in any form or by any means, mechanical or electronic, including photocopying or recording, or by any information storage and retrieval system, or transmitted by email without permission in writing from the publisher.

While all attempts have been made to verify the information provided in this publication, neither the author nor the publisher assumes any responsibility for errors, omissions or contrary interpretations of the subject matter herein.

This book is for entertainment purposes only. The views expressed are those of the author alone, and should not be taken as expert instruction or commands. The reader is responsible for his or her own actions.

Adherence to all applicable laws and regulations, including international, federal, state and local laws governing professional licensing, business practices, advertising and all other aspects of doing business in the US, Canada, UK or any other jurisdiction is the sole responsibility of the purchaser or reader.

Neither the author nor the publisher assumes any responsibility or liability whatsoever on the behalf of the purchaser or reader of these materials. Any perceived slight of any individual or organization is purely unintentional.

Contents

INTRODUCTION 1

CHAPTER 1: WHAT IS AN EMPATH? TRAITS & CATEGORIES OF EMPATHS 2

CHAPTER 2: HOW TO EMBRACE BEING AN EMPATH.........................9

CHAPTER 3: PRACTICAL BENEFITS OF BEING AN EMPATH 13

CHAPTER 4: THE STRUGGLES OF AN EMPATH 17

CHAPTER 5: COMMON MISCONCEPTIONS ABOUT BEING AN EMPATH 21

CHAPTER 6: LAYERS OF THE HUMAN ENERGY FIELD 25

CHAPTER 7: RAISING YOUR VIBRATION 29

CHAPTER 8: CHARACTERISTICS OF HIGHLY SENSITIVE PEOPLE.33

CHAPTER 9: TYPES OF ENERGY VAMPIRES.......................................37

CHAPTER 10: HOW TO SPOT AND PROTECT YOURSELF FROM ENERGY VAMPIRES 41

CHAPTER 11: HOW TO STOP ABSORBING OTHER PEOPLE'S ENERGY..45

CHAPTER 12: COPING STRATEGIES FOR HIGHLY SENSITIVE PEOPLE...49

CHAPTER 13: THINGS THAT HIGHLY SENSITIVE PEOPLE REQUIRE 53

CHAPTER 14: HOW TO DEAL WITH DIFFICULT PEOPLE AS A HIGHLY SENSITIVE PERSON 57

CHAPTER 15: HEALTH TIPS FOR HIGHLY SENSITIVE PEOPLE 61

CHAPTER 16: HOW TO AVOID ADDICTION AS AN EMPATH 65

CHAPTER 17: WAYS EMPATHS LOVE DIFFERENTLY 69

CHAPTER 18: WHY IS IT HARD FOR EMPATHS TO GET INTO SERIOUS RELATIONSHIPS? 73

CHAPTER 19: WHY EMPATHS AND NARCISSISTS ARE ATTRACTED TO EACH OTHER AND THE STAGES OF THEIR RELATIONSHIP 77

CHAPTER 20: IS YOUR CHILD AN EMPATH? TIPS FOR RAISING THEM 81

CHAPTER 21: BEST CAREER CHOICES FOR EMPATHS 85

CHAPTER 22: SIGNS YOU'RE AN INTUITIVE EMPATH – NOT JUST AN EMPATH 89

CHAPTER 23: HOW TO REMAIN IN BALANCE WITH YOUR EMOTIONS 93

CHAPTER 24: SIGNS YOU HAVE SPIRITUAL HEALING CAPABILITIES 97

CHAPTER 25: HOW TO STRENGTHEN YOUR MENTAL BODY 101

CHAPTER 26: WHAT IS A PSYCHIC EMPATH AND HOW TO TELL IF YOU'RE ONE? 105

CHAPTER 27: THE DIFFERENCE BETWEEN EMPATHS AND HIGHLY SENSITIVE PEOPLE 109

CHAPTER 28: HOW TO BOOST YOUR PSYCHIC ABILITIES 113

CONCLUSION 117

Introduction

You are standing next to your window, watching the world go by. You can see people walking down the street, old and young alike, each minding their own business. But you are sure of one thing – you're scared of being one of those people. If it were possible, you would rather spend the entire day in your apartment. In your experience, being around people can be extremely overwhelming because you seem to go through a roller coaster of emotions.

Each moment you spend out there, you are unsure of what emotion you will feel next. Frustration, excitement, grief, anxiety, joy, angst, annoyance, you name it. Thanks to your introspective mind, you have found out that you only feel these emotions when you are surrounded by people. And it's precisely why you have developed a tendency of running away from them every time you get overwhelmed.

There must be a deep cry from the depths of your soul – what am I?

You are an empath.

You have the special gift of soaking up the energies floating around you and perceiving them as though they were your own. Being an empath is a gift – not a curse. So it is high time you learned more about your capabilities.

Chapter 1: What is an Empath? Traits & Categories of Empaths

An empath is a person with the special gift of perceiving the emotions and feelings of other people as though they were their own. They don't even try. They are naturally tuned in to the energies floating around them. If an empath walks into a room and sits next to a person who's quietly mourning, the empath will pick up on the sorrow and experience it as though it were their own. An empath who lacks awareness of their gift can be deeply conflicted, as they cannot tell apart their own feelings from those of others.

Ask yourself the following questions to find out if you're an empath:

- o Can you perceive people in some way?
- o Do you feel people's emotions and mistake them as yours?
- o Can you think along the same line as other people?
- o Do your feelings change as soon as you meet a particular person?
- o Do you sometimes wonder whether you're co-dependent, neurotic, or even crazy?
- o Can you read peoples' minds?

It can be awesome having the ability to pick up on other people's energies, but on the downside, it can be a real struggle when the said energies are of the dark nature and especially if the empath in question knows nothing of their ability.

As an empath, these are some traits that you're bound to display:

Highly sensitive

People keep on telling you that you're too sensitive. This is because what they say or do can affect you quite easily. You can read into their unsaid messages when they talk or do something. This sensitivity can make you susceptible to things that don't hurt well-adjusted people. Your high sensitivity makes you give a lot of thought to what you do or say. This pattern always leads to self-inhibiting tendencies. You end up customizing yourself too much so that the world can fall in love with you. The habit of suppressing your true emotions comes with a cocktail of challenges.

Soak up other peoples' energies

You could be having a fantastic day with your spirits high, and then you go to Starbucks and sit next to a family who unbeknownst to you just lost one of their members. Nothing is said. All are sipping at their coffee with quiet faces. Ever so slowly, the joy you first had begins to fade away, and in its place, sadness takes over. You have no reason to be sad, but you experience this sadness anyway. Soon, the family gets up, troops out of Starbucks, and then your sadness fades away. You had just absorbed their energies.

Introverted

Being introverted is not the same as being shy. A shy person might loathe being alone and feel rejected for lack of human contact, but on the other hand, an introvert gets drained when they stay too long with other people, and they cherish being alone. A shy person has self-inhibiting tendencies, but an introvert has a strong sense of self and stays true to it. Empaths are more likely to be introverted than extroverted. They don't shun all human contact but prefer socializing on one-on-one terms, or within small groups.

Highly intuitive

One of the most effective weapons in an empath's hands is their gut feeling. They have this ability to sniff out the true nature of a situation. This makes it a bit hard to play games with an empath. They will see right through your tricks. As an empath, if you meet someone, you tend to have a gut feeling of what that person is really like. You are always in tune with your surroundings and can tell when there's danger. This ability is obviously one of the main advantages of being an empath because you're less likely to be taken for a ride.

Overwhelmed by relationships

Conventional relationships put emphasis on partners spending as much time together as possible. An empath cannot thrive in this kind of arrangement because they constantly pick up on their partner's emotions and mistake them as their own. This is not to say that empaths cannot form any relationships. However, the traditional arrangement of a relationship needs to be deconstructed. For instance, they can have a room of their own that they may retreat to when their urge to be alone kicks in, and also, their partners should be patient with them.

Take long to process emotions

The average person has a laser attention to their emotions. Whether sadness or joy, it kicks in suddenly. Their emotional reflexes are fast too. An empath takes the time to understand the emotions that they are currently feeling. For instance, if something terrible goes down, the sadness won't register immediately. They will first try to process the situation, going over the details time and again, and then the sadness will well up inside them. They can experience emotions in such a powerful way. Thus, whether it's sadness or joy, they feel it to the full.

Love nature

For most empaths, they are at their happiest when surrounded by nature. Whether it's the sunlight kissing their skin, the rain falling on them, or taking in a gulp of fresh air, no other activity restores their balance as being surrounded by the natural world. They feel a deep sense of connection with nature. When an empath is experiencing a tsunami of emotions, one of the restorative measures would be taking a stroll through an open area beneath the sky.

Strong senses

An empath boasts of very developed senses. They can catch the slightest whiff of an odor, can see into the shadows, can hear the tiniest sound, and can feel the vibrations of various other things. These developed senses make them so good at noticing the small stuff. Empaths seem to notice what would ordinarily escape the attention of most people. For this reason, they tend to flourish in careers that demand close attention and the exploration of the abstract.

Generous

There isn't a more selfless person than an empath. They don't have to have something in order to help. They are willing to go the extra mile and be of help. For instance, when an empath comes across a street child and sees their suffering, it tugs at their heart. They not only want to give them some food but also find a way of removing them from the streets. The majority of the world doesn't care about street children and see them as an annoyance. We can assume that the empaths of the world play a critical role in helping street children and other people who are experiencing hardship.

Creative

Empaths tend to be very creative. This is aided by the wealth of emotions that they are always experiencing. Their creative nature manifests itself in almost every aspect of their life — food, relationships, homes, and most importantly, career. An empath is likely to do well in a career in the arts. They have tremendous potential when it comes to drawing, writing, singing, or making films. They tend to portray their emotions unambiguously and can capture the emotions of other people just as intended.

People are drawn to you

If an empath isn't aware of their special gift, they are likely to hide away from the world. They would rather hide and be safe than stay among people and experience every emotion imaginable. This can make the society grow suspicious of them and even hate them. However, if an empath is self-aware and knows of their ability to soak up the energies floating around them, then people will be drawn to them. People know that empaths have a tremendous capacity of understanding them and helping them get through whatever challenges they are facing.

Empaths fall into the following distinct categories:

- o **Geomantic empaths**: These empaths are attuned to a certain environment or landscape. Geomantic empaths are connected to specific sites like buildings, lakes, oceans, and mountains. These empaths can feel the historical emotions of these sites. For instance, if an empath visits a site where people were slaughtered many years, they can still feel the sorrow. Empaths attach feelings to different environments so that each environment evokes certain emotions. Such empaths tend to carry souvenirs to remind them of various environments.
- o **Physical empaths**: Also known as a medical empath, they can pick up on the condition of someone else's body. They would instinctively know what ails another person. In extreme cases, they can pick up on the symptoms so that they share in the pain of the other person. Physical empaths also have healing abilities. They tend to take careers in conventional or alternative medicine. Physical empaths are great at taking care of ailing people. Those who have

ailments trust them instinctively because they can feel that they care.
- **Emotional empaths**: They are sensitive to the emotional energy floating around them. As an emotional empath, you will absorb the emotions of other people and think that they are yours. This can be deeply distressing if you're constantly around negative people. An emotional empath should increase their self-awareness so that they can tell apart their emotions from those of others. Emotional empaths tend to withdraw from other people so that they can spend time alone and recharge. An emotional empath should protect their energy by following various healing practices.
- **Animal empaths**: You have certainly seen someone in your neighborhood who is more interested in keeping company with animals than human beings. They have a certain pet or even various pets that mean the world to them. There's a high likelihood that such a person is an animal empath. An animal empath feels a deep connection toward animals. They can sense what the animals want or feel and the animals love them back. The connection is so deep that they have a way of communicating with each other. An animal empath answers to their intense desire of connecting with animals by domesticating their animals of choice. Also, they tend to be passionate about animal rights and make contributions to funds that advance animal welfare.
- **Plant empaths**: A plant empath shares a deep connection with a certain plant or plants in general. The plant evokes certain emotions when they touch it. A plant empath can communicate with the plant and can know its condition. They like hanging out near the plant in a natural environment, bringing it into their house, or planting it in the garden.
- **Precognitive empaths**: Are you the type of person that can always tell the future? And this is not down to your future alone, but also the future of other unrelated people or

events? You're certainly a precognitive empath. You tend to "see" things before they actually come to pass. Your visions are made manifest in various ways such as dreams or feelings. Having this ability to foresee the future is both rewarding and distressing. It can help you brace for the future, and at the same time, it can amplify your misery knowing the pain that awaits you.

- **Psychometric empaths**: This sort of empath has a deep connection to various physical objects. The physical objects arouse certain emotions in them. The objects could range from utensils, knives, jewelry, photos, etc., but they each awaken certain deep emotions when the person comes across them. For instance, if your dad handed down his knife to you and then died that same day, the knife could have a lot of sentimental value. Every time you come across such a knife, you would miss your dad terribly.
- **Telepathic empath**: A telepathic empath can know what is stored away in someone's mind. With a casual glance at that person, they can tell their unexpressed thoughts. This causes the empath to have too much insight into people and situations.

Chapter 2: How to Embrace Being an Empath

When you have the power of feeling, the emotions of other people is both a good thing and a bad thing. On the one hand, you can pick up on the positive energy and have a blast, but on the other hand, you can also pick up on the negative energy and have a miserable time of it. This is a deal breaker because there's much more negative energy in the world than positive energy.

If you're an empath, you can easily fall into the temptation of labeling your ability as a curse and locking yourself away in your own little world, but it doesn't have to be that way. You should instead embrace your special gift and use it to improve your life.

The following are ways of embracing your ability to bring out the best in you:

Find a space to restore your energy

Staying in contact with people for long amounts of time will drain your energy. To restore your energy, you must retreat into a quiet area. Improvise a place where you can retreat from time to time. This area should be well designed and shouldn't have any distractions.

Equip this area with the things that aid in acquiring peace of mind, such as music and light colors. For instance, you can create an extra room in your house for this purpose. When you come home from work, you can retreat into this place to recharge.

Run away from negative energy

If you have gotten past the stage of separating your emotions from the emotions of other people, you are in a position to identify the source of negative energy. Whenever you run into someone who's teeming with negative energy, you will obviously pick up on their energy. But you don't want to stick around and suffer needlessly. You should excuse yourself and walk away from the negative energy that they exude. This is not being selfish; it is an act of preserving your sanity. In this age of the internet, you don't have to be physically near a source of negative energy to experience it. That energy can reach you through social media or even email. So, make a point of blocking the people who are sources of negative energy online.

Have an outlet

What happens when you soak up the bad emotions of other people? You're left in a terrible state. It is worse if you lack awareness – as most empaths do – of your situation. You should engage in activities that help you shed off the negative energy. For instance, you could go to the gym, go out on a hike, or even volunteer in a charity organization. The purpose of doing these activities is to have an outlet for your emotions. If you give room to the negative emotions acquired from others, eventually your quality of life will come down.

Follow your dreams

When you're constantly picking up the energies of negative people, you are more susceptible to having a meltdown. However, instead of retreating into your shell and running away from people, you should apply your wealth of emotions in chasing your dreams. The more emotional depth you have, the large your reservoir of creativity. Tap into your emotions and put out something of great quality so that the world can celebrate you. For instance, if you're a writer, come up with a great screenplay. Explore your emotions through the characters. The world will appreciate that. And what's more? You could make a fortune!

Show gratitude

Being an empath is not a curse! Many people have it worse! How about showing some gratitude? The more appreciative you are of the life that you have at present, the better your life will become. Being grateful is a key element of cultivating the right mindset, and it opens you up to more ways of making your life better. Also, when you're grateful, you will naturally cultivate partnerships with people. You have a far much better chance of achieving success when you have a huge network than when you're running alone.

Reach out to other empaths

If you're an empath, you must have gotten tired of people telling you that you're too sensitive. You read into tiny details about everything and have a rigid way of doing your activities. You almost feel like an alien amongst human beings because no one seems to understand you. But that shouldn't be the case. You can surely find people – empaths – who are your kindred spirits. If you know of none in your area of residence, you can search online communities, and you will surely find a community that caters to empaths. When you find your family, finally you will experience a sense of belonging and life won't be as hard as it first seemed. You can go on ahead to give one another much-needed encouragement.

Meditate

We really underestimate the usefulness of meditation. This ancient-old practice is critical in restoring balance to your mind and spirit. As an empath, you should take to meditation to flush out negative energy and improve your mind and spirit. If you meditate regularly, you will have the mental stamina to get through the day without being critically affected by the emotions of other people. Meditation will help you cultivate a strong identity of self.

Understand that it's okay not to fit in

Some empaths view their ability as a burden, not a special gift, and this affects them tremendously. It can result in them shutting out the world. This brings unwanted attention to them. People react by thinking that something is questionable about the empath and treat them with suspicion. Society ends up treating such empaths as outcasts. Empaths should be proud of their special gift and embrace with pride their quirky features instead of locking themselves away. If they openly celebrate their quirkiness, society won't treat them as outcasts.

Chapter 3: Practical Benefits of Being an Empath

The following are some benefits that come with being an empath:

Ability to detect lies

If you have some experience, you should know that human beings are not very truthful. They have an almost innate need to lie. As an empath, you know immediately when someone tells you a lie. You will only give them one glance and know – either from their body language or through intuition – that they have told a lie. This can really help you navigate through life while avoiding figurative minefields in the form of falsehoods. Being able to detect lies helps you save time and also achieve your important life goals.

Creativity

As an empath, you are very expressive. This ability helps you to succeed in every work situation since you have a touch of creativity. Empaths tend to flourish in careers that call on creativity, particularly the arts. This creative streak helps you attract a massive number of followers, land exclusive opportunities, and meet important people. Being creative is critical even in sustaining relationships. Many relationships fail not because the partners are not suited for each other, but simply because the partners – the husband, especially – is a boring rooster with zero imagination.

People confide in you

Let's face it: most people are ruthless. Nobody has time to waste paying attention to the problems of another. Enter the empath – a person who not only has the time to listen to your problems but is also willing to assist you in getting rid of them. When people come across such an accommodating person, they are drawn to them because they are sincere. People have confidence in an empath, and they usually divulge their hidden secrets to them. It's always a good thing when people trust you because it lays the foundation for helping one another.

Animals are drawn to you

Numerous studies have confirmed what empaths always knew — that animals have feelings. Animals can tell a good person from a bad person. If you mean an animal harm, they will try to escape from you long before you make your intention clear. Empaths have nothing but love toward animals. They share a connection. For this reason, animals are drawn toward empaths. Empaths have tender feelings toward all creatures.

Pick up on positive vibes

Being an emotional empath means that you will pick up on the vibes that people give off. Most empaths focus on the negative side of their ability; the fact that they will soak up negative energy. But on the brighter side, they can soak up positive energy as well. This means that if they hang out near positive people, their current emotional state doesn't matter, but they will feel positive too. Empaths should prioritize hanging out near positive people so that they can take advantage of this default arrangement. Meeting positive people on a consistent basis can be quite challenging, but just as with anything else, you can pull this off with enough determination.

Huge capacity to express love

When two people are in a relationship, one of the challenges that they face is to understand each other. They may not often come to a common ground. As an empath, you can understand someone at a deeper level. This ability allows you to express your love and commitment to your partner in an unparalleled manner. Your partner will have a huge appreciation for your ability to understand them, and it will inspire them to become an even better partner. As they say, it takes real effort on the part of both partners to make a relationship work.

Healing capabilities

Empaths have the ability to cure people of various afflictions. When an ailment is made manifest in the physical realm, it means that the spiritual realm is not well aligned. For the ailment to go away, the spiritual realm will have to be healed first. Empaths have this natural restorative potential. An empath can help restore the spiritual realm into perfect balance, and by extension, help that person get rid of the ailment dogging them. Thus, empaths are said to have healing capabilities by virtue of their restorative powers.

Appreciate beauty

An empath has a tremendous capacity to appreciate beauty. They have an innate ability to see the perfection in both small and big things in life. What may look ordinary to the average pair of eyes might indeed be a work of intense beauty to the empath. For this reason, empaths are drawn to authentic and organically-formed things. They don't appreciate shiny things because they know it's likely that the quality has been compromised. For an empath, beauty runs through all things in existence.

Stay away from trouble

You would have to be superhuman to deflect all manner of troubles. But still, having the ability to sense what a person is like from just meeting them, coupled with the ability to foretell what will go down in the future, inspires you to protect yourself. If your intuition tells you that a person is dangerous, you will obviously stay away from them; thus, avoiding trouble. If you have dreamed about something terrible taking place in the future, you can take action at present that will mitigate the impact of the problem or eliminate it altogether.

No need for being fake

Nothing repels an empath more than fake things or fake people. So, naturally, they wouldn't want to be what they detest. An empath wants to be authentic about every aspect of their life. This makes them appear grounded, mature, and deeply creative. In a world plagued with fake things and fake people, a sense of originality is welcome.

When happy, they are enormously happy

This goes back to an empath's ability to savor their emotions comprehensively. They experience every emotion to its last bit. If it is pain, they feel it deeply, but if it is happiness, they feel it just as deeply. This is great because it allows them to be exceedingly happy while it lasts.

Chapter 4: The Struggles of an Empath

The following are some struggles that empaths endure:

Trouble watching TV

Television is one of the most popular entertainment media. At any given time, there are hundreds of millions of eyeballs glued to the TV. Sadly, TV is full of content that scares away empaths. Things like cruelty, tragedy, and violence tend to repel them. Empaths can only watch TV for a limited time to catch up with the programs that are not violence-ridden and that nourish their sensitive souls.

Trouble saying NO

An empath is terribly sensitive and hates having to disappoint other people. If someone asks an empath for a favor, the empath will find themselves saying 'Yes' even though it would inconvenience them. This causes them to have a hard time of it because they took responsibilities that they were not ready or willing to perform. An empath's inability to say 'No' results in problems and ultimately lowers the quality of their life. To learn to say 'No' without feeling guilty, the empath will have to acquire assertive skills.

Hate leaving the house

Empaths want to stay in their rooms for as long as humanly possible because once they step out, they will encounter people, and then they will start soaking up the energies of these people. The thought of leaving the house is a bit scary to an empath. However, they have to step out of the house because it is not practical to stay indoors all the time. Empaths have to learn measures of protecting their energy while they are out. One of these measures includes visualizing a protective shield of light around their body.

Super sensitive

Empaths are terribly sensitive. In social gatherings, they have a hard time fitting in because they are scrutinizing every word that is being said. They are conscious of what they say too and how they behave in front of others. This is what contributes to their awkward behavior when in public. Also, thanks to their sensitive nature, they tend to smell trouble where there is none. For instance, if they greet someone and the person fails to answer back, they start imagining that the said person hates them. But they don't stop to consider that their voice is small and nervous and that the person never heard them in the first place – that's why they didn't answer back.

They are easily overwhelmed

For an empath, there's nothing more taxing than being out in public alone. Whether they are in the mall, gym, or supermarket, they experience a myriad of emotions which make them overwhelmed. This state makes them uncomfortable and nervous. It is upon an empath to adopt strategies that will help them tell apart the energies from those of others, and more importantly, guard their energy.

Lack of friends

An empath is quick to see fake people. Sadly, true friends are rare. Most empaths would rather stay alone than have fake friends. Their sensitive nature makes them easily give up looking for true friends. So, they may end without anyone to spend time with. The fact that empaths are not huge on mixing with people, it becomes even harder to make friends. In as much as empaths treasure their alone time, it doesn't mean that they hate making friends. They would love to have friends just like everybody, but the problem is that the said friends are parasites, really.

Mood swings

As an empath, getting bombarded with a range of emotions as you progress through the day will affect your moods. Your moods will change depending on the kind of energy you run into. If you run into hateful people, your mood will turn dark, and if you run into positive people, you will lighten up. To have stable moods, it is imperative that you take up measures of keeping your energy steady. It is not a simple exercise. You will have to practice over and over again to get it right.

Hard to connect with other people

It is one thing to have friends, and it is another to connect with them on a deep level. An empath may have a difficult time connecting with other people because their sensitive nature makes them not trust people easily. Ordinarily, it takes an empath a long time to trust anyone, unlike other people who seem to trust others in an instant. When you have a hard time trusting people, you will hardly open up to them which hurts your ability to connect with them. Empaths need to work on their ability to trust others.

They tend to complicate relationships

Being in a relationship with an empath can be trying. For one, they are deeply sensitive. Their partner must think and rethink their words and actions because the empath can catch the wrong meaning and get hurt. After a while, this starts to become tiring. Also, considering the empath's tendency of soaking up other people's emotions, you may find them declining to spend time with you. They will occasionally pull away from your embrace and go into a secluded area to recharge their energy. This can be deeply frustrating especially if you're the type that loves spending a lot of time with your partner.

They attract energy vampires

Empaths draw energy vampires to them like moths to light. Energy vampires operate at a low vibration, and they can spot empaths from a mile off, and when they do, they come running in to suck the energy out of them. Energy vampires are great at mimicking good behavior, but it is not long before the empath catches up to their fallacy. Energy vampires cause great damage to empaths because they not only drain them of energy but also make them feel guilty when they try to pull away.

Chapter 5: Common Misconceptions About Being an Empath

There are various myths perpetuated about empaths that are simply not true. The following are some common fallacies about being an empath:

Empaths are weak

This is the biggest misconception about empaths. As an empath, you can absorb the energies that other people put out – isn't that some sort of superpower? Then, consider the fact that empaths have to process all these emotions barging into their minds from outside and you will see it takes incredible stamina not to cave in. An empath may be highly sensitive and may even cry when they experience melancholia, but that doesn't mean that you can break them at will. Empaths are strong people. This strength is made manifest in their ability to soak up a range of emotions throughout the day and still keep their sanity. Empaths have a strong capacity to withstand the wave of negative emotions constantly hitting them, and this capacity is a testament to their mental strength. Their tendency to experience meltdowns is not down to the fact that they are weak; rather, it stems from their highly sensitive nature. An empath intensely experiences the world, and they can feel every ounce of energy wrapped in a word or an action. For this reason, their emotions are greatly influenced by what people say or do, and they might misconstrue the intended message. For instance, if a man stares wildly at an empath, the empath's heart might start racing, thinking that the man means them harm. Whereas, the truth is that the man hasn't even noticed the empath yet, and is only staring into the vacuous space in front of him, lost in his thoughts.

Empaths consider themselves special

As an empath, you are wont to creating high standards for yourself. These standards will be made manifest in both your career goals and personal life. For instance, if you're looking for a life partner, there are certain features that you will require of them. If those features are absent, then that's a deal breaker. Obviously, you can only settle when you meet a life partner with the features that you consider important. However, for the other people looking in from the outside, you will seem stuck up and entitled. They might say that you have too high an opinion of yourself and that's why you haven't settled down yet; that you expect to be treated as though you were someone special. Empaths are not entitled. But they tend to have high standards about the things that they want from life. Whether it is material things, relationships or friendships, they must align with their requirements and this rigid expectation can come off as holding themselves above the rest.

Empaths are drawn to narcissists hoping that they will change them

The narcissist is such a complex animal. They have so many tricks under their hat; it's amazing. When a narcissist comes into your life, they give no sign that something is wrong with them. You start out with them while they are perfect, and as time goes, the complications begin. They begin small before their true nature comes out. When a narcissist wants to draw an empath, they first make a point of knowing what the empath is looking for. When they have done their assignment, and become aware of what the empath is looking for, they start to project these qualities. If the empath fails to see right through the fakeness of the narcissist, they fall into their trap. It is not true at all that the empath gets into a relationship with the narcissist with the idealistic notion of wanting to save the narcissist. The empath is merely a victim of the narcissist. When the narcissist peels back the mask so that their true self shines through, the empath is thrown into confusion, struggling to make sense of whatever is happening.

Empaths are cold and unfeeling

Empaths who are not yet aware of their special gift tend to lead sad lives. They may lock themselves away and shun the world. They lack the awareness that they can soak up other people's energies so that they perceive them as their own. This causes them to clam up and act as though they are not interested in the world. People might see such an empath and conclude that they are cold and unfeeling. They couldn't be further from the truth. Regardless of their facial expression, an empath is at all times processing an emotion. Beneath their seemingly cold exterior, there is a sensitive world holding a wealth of emotions. As for the empowered empath, they know too well when to pull away from human contact to recharge their energy. The empowered empath has no qualms about mixing with people and having a great time, but the difference is that they know when to pull away.

Empaths are mentally ill

Another huge misconception is that empaths are suffering from some form of mental illness. Aside from this being a misconception, it is also somewhat offensive. Empaths have to struggle with having to soak up the emotions of other people and this can make them seem quirky, but it doesn't make them mentally ill. The mental health of empaths must be very high, especially when you consider the fact that they can still put their life together despite the constant waves of emotions that keep sneaking up on them. Clearly, empaths are not suffering from any mental illness.

Empaths are lazy

Another misconception is the idea that empaths are lazy. It's true that when an empath endures a never-ending streak of emotional intrusion from an external source, they can become inactive, but this should not be attributed to laziness. In most cases, it is a condition known as Chronic Fatigue Syndrome. Also, having to put up with energy vampires will drain an empath of their mental, emotional, and physical energy.

Chapter 6: Layers of the Human Energy Field

Human beings are actually multi-dimensional. We are composed of layers of energy that extend into realms beyond the physical plane. These layers of energy are critical in helping us express the full range of the vibrations that we experience.

The following are the energy layers that a human being is composed of:

Physical body

The physical body is the first layer of energy. It is essentially what we perceive as parts of our body. Although our bodies are made up of various organs and systems, at the basic level, all these organs comprise energy. So our physical body is really an expression of certain vibrations.

Etheric body

The etheric body is the second layer. It basically refers to the state that is between matter and energy. It is located approximately a quarter inch from the physical body. The etheric layer of energy is modeled after the physical body, and it is grayish. The etheric body tends to move around in wavy motions. The etheric body is a huge influence on the structure of the physical body, and it informs various patterns of the physical body. The etheric body is what holds the physical body intact.

Emotional body

This layer of energy is lighter when compared to the etheric body. It caters to the emotions that a human being experiences. The emotional layer of energy exudes a wide range of colors, unlike the etheric body which gives off gray only. The emotional body oscillates very often through a variety of colors, unlike the etheric body which is pretty rigid. Depending on the extremity of the emotions that a person goes through, the color of their emotional body can go from bright to dark. The emotional body can interpenetrate both the etheric and physical bodies.

The mental body

The mental body caters to the thought processes that individuals have. The mental body has a distinct yellow form that surrounds the whole person but is mainly concentrated around the head and shoulders. The mental body is made of a lighter auric substance than both the emotional and etheric bodies. The mental body is situated about ten inches from the physical body, but it widens depending on the intensity of a person's mental activity. The mental body has a structure, and various thought forms can be perceived. The mental body is interdependent with the emotional body. Various thought forms are illuminated with distinct colors. When a person has a clear thought, and there's no noise on their mind, their thought form will seem bright. But when they are experiencing cloudy judgment, and there's too much fog in their mind, their thought form will appear dark. The mental body is more fluid than both the emotional and etheric bodies. This is because the average person is always engaging their brain in interpreting the world surrounding them. The mental body plays a critical role in the auric field and has a trickledown effect on other layers of energy.

The astral body

The astral body is the center of transformation and transition. The lower levels of the auric field relate to the functions and processes inherent to the physical experience. However, the upper levels of the auric field relate to the functions and processes of the non-physical experience. The astral body provides a gateway between the physical and the non-physical. The astral body doesn't have any definite structure, but just like the emotional body, it features a wide array of colors to express various forms. The astral body is situated about one foot away from the physical body. The colors of the astral body have a better aesthetic quality than those of the emotional body. Additionally, the astral body contains a rose element that is connected to the heart chakra or the state of being in love. Much of the non-physical interaction between people happens at the astral level of energy. People with clairvoyant abilities can observe balls of energy shifting between people, even though the people involved aren't actually interacting. For instance, if two people have intense feelings toward each other such as love or anger, blobs of energy can be seen through the astral level shifting back and forth between them.

The etheric template body

The etheric template body is situated about two feet from the physical body. This template plays a critical role in the formation of the etheric layer, and by extension, the physical body. There is a template that looks like the physical body that exists at the etheric layer. The etheric template plays the role of informing the etheric body. The etheric template creates space upon which the etheric auric field may exist. The etheric template is critical in building the grid where the physical energy manifests.

The celestial body

The celestial body is the auric field that allows us to experience universal love and soul-enriching consciousness. It is the emotional form of the spiritual grid. Love for humanity is processed in both the astral body and the heart chakra, but the celestial body makes it possible to experience universal love. The celestial body helps us unite with all things in existence and see ourselves as an extension of the universe – not an independent entity. The celestial body extends to about two and three-quarters feet from the physical body and is far lighter than the etheric template layer.

The ketheric template or causal body

The ketheric template is situated around three and a half feet from the physical body. The ketheric template plays a protective role over all the other bodies in the auric field. It is the final auric layer in the human energy field and plays a significant role in outlining the path that an individual will follow throughout their life. This body of energy is made of extremely light substance, and the golden color is dominant. People with clairvoyant abilities can spot shimmers of golden spears of light around a person. The ketheric template is critical in understanding your consciousness, as well as matters touching upon your past lives.

Chapter 7: Raising Your Vibration

Change is the only constant. At every moment, you are either acting or reacting to life, and the result is either an increase or decrease in your vibration. Every action or interaction throughout your life will affect your energy levels. If you make good choices, you increase your vibration, and conversely, if you make bad choices, you lower your vibration. You need to be full of energy to experience a high frequency. If your energy is drained, you will experience low vibrations, and as a result, your mental, spiritual, and physical bodies will suffer.

As an empath, you are at risk of getting your energy drained mostly by energy vampires. So, you must get proficient at raising your vibrations so that you won't suffer through the negative experience that comes with low frequencies such as stagnation, lethargy, negativity, and health complications. You also need to have a higher vibration to be complete and enjoy your life to the maximum.

The following are some tips you can take to raise your frequency:

Cut off toxic friends

They say that you're the average of the five people that you spend most of your time with. Following this premise, we can deduce that spending time with positive people will make you a positive person, just as spending time with negative people will make you a negative person. Learn to recognize people in your circles with toxic personalities and get rid of them before you absorb their character. When you cut off negative people from your life, you give yourself a chance to accumulate the energy you require to bloom. Their negativity would have hindered you from making decisions that will fulfill you.

Cleanse your body

It is easy to poison our bodies through what we consume. If you don't watch your diet, you could very easily accumulate harmful substances in your body, resulting in unpleasant consequences. To raise your vibration, you have to have a clean and healthy body. First, eliminate toxins from your body, and moving on, watch what you eat. There are various ways of eliminating toxins from your body, and you will have to find the one that suits you. Some methods will require professional guidance and others can be done on your own. To keep toxins at a minimum, ensure that you have a balanced diet and consume lots of fruits and vegetables.

Exercise

People who exercise regularly are in a much better physical condition than people who don't exercise at all. As an empath, you need to have the mental and emotional strength to visualize a protective membrane around you so that vampires won't deplete your energy. Exercise improves heart health and helps your body perform various functions optimally. If you start exercising regularly, your body cells will become strong, and you will have more energy to devote to your daily activities. You are much more likely to achieve your important life goals with a healthy body than when your health is failing.

Meditate

Meditation is another great way of raising your vibration. It is a great method of releasing tension and calming down the noise in your mind. When you eliminate the noise from your mind, you are in a much better position to take decisions and make progress. Meditation improves both the emotional and physical state of a person. The more emotionally grounded you are, the higher your chances of achieving success.

Journal

Writing down your thoughts is an underestimated way of raising your vibration. When you put your thoughts onto paper, you give yourself a chance to heal from the troubling experiences that you have been through. Journaling has a therapeutic effect. More importantly, journaling will help you notice the pattern for your energy drain. For instance, if your energy gets drained around particular people, places, or periods, you will know. You will have insight into how you relate to various external factors. This awareness can help you make conscious decisions to alleviate your suffering and promote wellness.

Be kind and generous

Some people seem to equate kindness or generosity to a person's ability to fork out money. Actually, the biggest resource that you could ever give is your time and affection. Learn to extend a helping hand to those who are in need. If you make the lives of other people easy, you will have a sense of pride, and it will increase your zest for life. When you're in a great emotional state, you are less likely to cave into negativity and other nasty complications attached to low vibrations. Get into the habit of practicing kindness, and it will improve your emotional state.

Watch what you feed your mind

If you feed your mind with negativity, you will lower your vibration, and if you feed your mind with positivity, you will raise your vibration. Guard closely the types of media you expose yourself to. For instance, don't develop the habit of watching TV programs that promote violence. For an empath, watching violence would drain your energy and cause you to function at a low frequency. In this age of the internet, terrible and dehumanizing media is just a few clicks away, and you may want to stay away from that.

Music

Music is a great way of raising your frequency. When you listen to soothing music, it tends to carry away your worries and refreshes your spirit. Obviously, you want to listen to music that is positive or the type that caters to your idea of entertainment. If your energy has been drained as a result of mixing with energy vampires, raise your vibration back up by listening to positive music. The music will practically lift your energy levels. When you are feeling refreshed, you are in the best headspace to confront life.

Chapter 8: Characteristics of Highly Sensitive People

A highly sensitive person has an intense cognitive processing toward emotional, mental, and physical stimuli. This makes them react to things in different ways than well-adjusted people. The following are some traits that highly sensitive people exhibit:

Easily overwhelmed

A highly sensitive person is easily overwhelmed by different stimuli. For instance, they can't handle staying in environments with too much noise or light. They are sensitive to the extra noise and light. Sensitive people like establishing familiarity with things first before they start using them habitually. This makes them appear odd in front of other well-adjusted people.

Take a lot of time to complete tasks

It can be a real nightmare for a sensitive person to be required to complete a task within a limited amount of time. Sensitive people like taking their time when performing a task. Their mental activity is vigorous. Their thoughts shoot off in a dozen ways, and they have a hard time reconciling the fact that they have to deliver perfect results and time is limited. Sensitive people can hardly perform when they are subjected to a lot of pressure. For this reason, they do well in artistic careers like designing than high-pressure careers like news reporting.

They like staying alone

The average person likes to mix with other people in order not to feel alone. However, a sensitive person likes staying alone. This doesn't mean that they close off human ties altogether. They might keep a small group of friends for their socializing needs. Sensitive people like retreating into solitude because they get drained when they spend time with others. They can perceive the thoughts and energies of other people around them and actually soak up these energies. Their ability to absorb other peoples' energies forces them to isolate themselves so that they don't have to go through that again.

Extremely observant

The average person only ever sees the obvious. For instance, when the average person walks into their boss' office, they might take notice of only their dress style. However, a sensitive person would go deeper into the subtleties. They would notice the color of the clothes, the type of shoes, the angle of the boss's eyes, the smell, and so on. Sensitive people have sharp observation skills. They are the first to notice an anomaly or notice a deviation from the norm.

Cannot function well when over-aroused

A sensitive person has to first get over their arousal before they can function in a normal way. For instance, if they receive extremely elating news, they are forced to stop doing whatever they are doing and concentrate on celebrating. They can only go back to the right headspace for work once they have gotten over the exciting news. If a sensitive person were forced to work while they were in an aroused state, they'd surely not perform. To minimize such cases, sensitive people have to get rid of things that may stimulate them when they are supposed to be busy.

Can read the minds and moods of other people

The average, well-adjusted person can hardly read the mind of other people, but a sensitive person would only have to glance at a person, and they'd read their mind. This special ability helps them anticipate what other people are about to say or do – and in most cases, they are right. Sensitive people are very intuitive, and they rely on this gift to detect the vibrations of those around them. Thus, they can read not only other peoples' minds but moods too.

Very imaginative

A sensitive person has a childlike sense of wonder inside them. They are always poring through things in their minds. Banking on their wealth of emotions, a sensitive person has a rich imagination which they tap into when needed. A sensitive person is far more likely to come up with a creative solution to a problem than a non-sensitive individual. Their creativity makes them suitable for careers in the arts. They tend to flourish where there are no conventional rules, and there's permission to express oneself as their imagination dictates.

Very philosophical

Sensitive people tend to ask deep, philosophical questions. The world presents this huge mystery, and they have to try to understand the world through a philosophical perspective. A sensitive person will have questions, such as where did humans come from? Why are we here? What is our destiny? Their philosophical mind stretches from wanting to find answers about human existence to all other aspects of life. They may have a philosophy touching upon sexuality, society, and the education system. Sensitive people also tend to read a lot in an attempt to explain away their deep unanswered questions.

Comprehend human emotions better than other people

Human emotions can be quite confusing. The average person may not be able to understand their own emotions or the emotions of other people. It doesn't matter how these emotions are well explained; you may find yourself not fully comprehending the depth or nature of a person's emotions. However, when it comes to a sensitive person, they are very good at decoding the exact feelings of a person. Sometimes, they don't even have to be told, as they can deduce for themselves by just looking at what the person in question has been through. For instance, if someone's parents have been murdered, the person will obviously go into mourning. However, a sensitive person can perceive precisely how devastated the person feels.

Can stay still for long periods of time

A sensitive person can stay still for an extended period of time provided there are no distractions. This ability allows them to be incredibly focused when performing a task. But then they don't necessarily have to be working. A sensitive person can plop down onto a seat and stay still for a long period of time without engaging in any activity whatsoever. This is difficult for the average person considering that they need constant human contact.

Chapter 9: Types of Energy Vampires

Victim vampire

The victim vampire is the type of person who thinks that they are at the mercy of the world. They have a long list of people who did "wrong by them", and they believe that were it not for these people, their lives would have been better. Everyone is scheming against them. When you come into contact with a victim vampire, they will make it seem as though your actions or words have affected their lives. They will make you the villain.

Innocent vampire

Not all energy vampires are malicious people. Some energy vampires can actually be people you care about. In most cases, they are people that have valid reasons to depend on you. For instance, if your spouse suffers an accident and they have to rely on you, or your little sibling hasn't stopped being needy, or your parents are always checking after you. It is okay to help these people with whatever they demand of you, but at the same time, you should put plans in place to ensure that they become self-dependent as soon as humanly possible.

Narcissistic vampire

A narcissist cannot show empathy. They tend to sneak up on you by wearing a mask, a false identity, and when you drop your guard, their true nature comes out. A narcissist only cares about their own needs. They will stop at nothing to ensure that they have snatched whatever they wanted from you. A narcissist gets very delighted whenever they spot an empath because they know empaths are easy to exploit. They will drain you of energy, thanks to their parasitic nature. Once a narcissist is done using you, they will get rid of you.

Dominator vampire

This kind of vampire tries to get involved in every aspect of your life by being overbearing. They want to influence your life down to the smallest detail. When you leave them out on any decision that you make, they act angry toward you. Their intense desire to dominate others stems from a point of insecurity. They are afraid of being seen as weak. Empaths are easy targets because of their sensitive nature. A dominator vampire will suffocate you with their presence and a never-ending desire to be the architect of your life, and for this reason, they will drain you of energy.

Melodramatic vampire

Melodramatic vampires are great at creating scenes. They always drag you into trouble that would have been avoided easily by observing basic rules of decency. You could be out having a fun time, and then they will start a fight with someone random and put you into danger. What's really happening with a melodramatic vampire is that they feel empty in their souls. They have nothing to live for and thus creating drama becomes their second nature.

Melodramatic vampires are very determined, but if you want to get rid of them, you have to be particularly ruthless.

Judgmental vampire

These kinds of vampires thrive on passing judgments on everything that you do. They intend to make you feel bad about your decisions or actions. For instance, if you buy a present for your loved one, the judgmental vampire might spread malicious rumors about you having to buy love. They are intent on tarnishing your reputation and making you seem bad. Empaths are sensitive, and when someone judges their deeds, they feel underwhelmed. An empath should stay away from judgmental people to avoid getting their feelings hurt, and by extension, suffering energy drain.

Blamer vampire

The blamer vampire can never accept personal responsibility for what is wrong in their life. For instance, if you accompany your friend to apply for college and their application fails, and then they blame you for somehow making their application fail to get through, they are certainly blamer vampires. A blamer vampire refuses to take charge of their own life and finds people to blame for what's wrong with their life. A blamer vampire will not do things alone. They delegate work to victims. If things go to the dogs, they whip out the blame card, but should their plan pan out — they will bask in the glory.

Jealous vampire

The jealous vampire will never be happy for anyone. It doesn't stop there either. They will try to hurt anyone that they think is doing better than them. The jealous person will try to devise a plan to harm a person, and they leave that person devastated. For instance, if you get someone to agree to become your significant other, a jealous person might contact them and say some untrue things and end up tarnishing your name, making your significant other view you in a suspicious light. The jealous vampire relishes seeing people in pain.

Whining vampires

It is not only tiring being around this people but annoying as well. When they encounter the least challenge, their knee-jerk reaction is to whine and cry about it, rather than take helpful actions. When you stay close to a person who's eternally whining, their negativity eventually closes up on you and causes your vibrations to go down. Whining vampires influence you into developing negative thoughts and this stifles your ability to make progress. Empaths should note people who have a tendency of whining and eliminate them from their lives.

Insecurity vampires

Some people are so insecure about themselves that they end up becoming energy vampires. The problem with being insecure is that it makes you look for ways to overcompensate. For instance, if a short man is insecure about their height, they might develop a queer habit of making their selves look bigger. They will come across as a try hard, and this behavior will hinder them from having normal interactions with other people. When a person reeks of insecurity, other people tend to be wary of them. This leads to the parties engaging in wars and counter wars at the emotional and astral level.

Chapter 10: How to Spot and Protect Yourself from Energy Vampires

Have you ever gone somewhere feeling vibrant and after spending time around that place, you felt drained of energy? Or have you ever met someone and after spending time with them, you felt an energy drain? Both of these situations point to an encounter with an energy vampire. Most energy vampires are only interested in their own desires, lack empathy, and are incredibly immature. An energy vampire will leave you feeling exhausted, irritated, and overwhelmed. An energy vampire can be anyone – friends, family, coworkers, etc. Once you realize that someone is a vampire, you should do yourself a favor and cut them off from your life. Getting rid of an energy vampire is not a self-serving deed; it is an act of self-preservation. The vibrations of energy, vampires are incredibly low. As a coping strategy, they have to suck energy from others through the following ways:

- **Gossiping**: An energy vampire knows that people want to hear a good story. So, they say anything in an attempt to earn the attention of their victim. They resort to telling lies about people. If an energy vampire tells you about other people, you can be sure that they will tell other people about you as well. They also start slow wars between factions by telling each side antagonizing news.
- **Manipulation**: An energy vampire is a master manipulator. Before they approach anyone, they already have a script to play by and have rehearsed how to take advantage of that person. They have no remorse about manipulating people into doing their bidding, as their capacity to empathize is incredibly limited. Energy vampires get a high out of manipulating people and getting their way.
- **Complaining**: No one is more "wronged" in the entire world. An energy vampire believes that the world is out to get them. They can take advantage of someone and yet find a way of twisting the story so that they appear to be the victims. An energy vampire is good at weaving stories together, and they have the experience of passing themselves off as victims. Due to this habit of complaining, an energy vampire tends to be slack in their work, knowing too well they can find something to complain about or someone to throw the blame at.
- **Massive ego**: An energy vampire has a massive ego, and it comes with delusions of grandeur. An energy vampire sets themselves extremely ambitious goals. The goals are unrealistic because they lack the wherewithal of achieving these goals. Their massive ego also manifests in how they treat other people. Energy vampires think that they are special people and are above everyone else. Thus, they act self-entitled and expect everyone to bow down to them. When an energy vampire comes into your life, they will normally have an agenda of taking something away from you, before they move on to the next victim.

- **Not being accountable**: An energy vampire will hardly ever be accountable for anything. They want easy things and hate responsibility. Due to this hatred of accountability, energy vampires make the worst candidates for doing any serious task. They will usually disappoint you. If you have to rely on an energy vampire for the completion of a task, they will frustrate you with their subpar performance and an unwillingness to be accountable. Energy vampires will develop a hatred toward anyone that expects them to be answerable, but when the shoe is on the other foot, they are extremely ruthless.
- **Neglecting the needs of their dependents:** Energy vampires are only interested in their own needs and woe unto anyone that depends on them. For instance, if the energy vampire in question has a family, they may spend their earnings on vain things like sex and alcohol at the expense of their family. The people that depend on an energy vampire lead very sad lives because of both the cruelty and humiliation that the energy vampire metes out at them. More often than not, children raised by energy vampires turn into social misfits because they have known nothing but pain their whole lives.

When an energy vampire is around you, you will feel uneasy, and soon your energy levels will take a massive dip. The following are some things that take place when attacked by an energy vampire:

- **Nausea**: After an interaction with an energy vampire, you can be left feeling nauseous. This feeling may be accompanied by a stomach ache. This happens because your body is going through a lot of stress because of losing energy. Once you get rid of the energy vampire, both the nausea and the stomach ache will go away.
- **Headache**: An energy vampire will also make you experience a terrible headache. Once your energy levels go down, there's not enough energy for your brain. The brain reacts

by trying to create awareness of the fact that the body has run out of sugars. The brain consumes a significant portion of the total energy of a person, and if the energy suffers a drop, a person's ability to use their mental faculties is severely affected.

Once you find out that someone is an energy vampire, the ultimate remedy is to cut the person out of your life. However, in some instances, you're stuck with them because they play an indispensable role in your life. The following are tips to help you cope against attacks from energy vampires:

- **Set boundaries**: Let the person know that you have boundaries that are not to be crossed. This limits the time that you get to spend around the energy vampire.
- **Recite positive mantras**: Mantras are short phrases that a person says over and over with the intention of reaffirming a particular belief. Create more positive energy for yourself by reciting mantras.
- **Visualization**: Using your mind's eye, visualize a membrane of light around your body, shielding your energy from loss. This will greatly reduce the amount of energy lost to the vampire.

Chapter 11: How to Stop Absorbing Other People's Energy

Having the ability to soak up other people's energy would be great if we lived in Utopia. Sadly, we live on Earth, and most people harbor more negativity than positivity. Being around people, you are going to feel negative, not because you are negative yourself, but because you have picked up on their energy. Obviously, you want to get past this condition. The following are some tips to help you stop absorbing other peoples' energy:

Walk away

Walking away is not as easy as it seems. First, you have to tell apart your own emotions from those of others. An empath tends to mistakenly think that they have negative thoughts when it is the energy vampire near them channeling those negative thoughts, and by the time they realize, the damage is done. So, you have to perfect your capability to detect an energy vampire very quickly and move away from them. If you go away from an energy vampire, you won't suffer more loss.

Meditate

Meditating is a perfect way of increasing your state of aliveness. It refreshes your mind and affords you plenty more energy. The more you meditate, the more you flex both your mental and spiritual muscle. Eventually, you become so developed that you acquire certain mental powers that are alien to normal people. To maximize the effectiveness of meditation, you have to conduct it in the best environment. The best place to conduct meditation is a serene and non-polluted area. Take deep breaths and exhale in a calculated way. Focus on clearing away the noise in your mind and heightening your self-awareness.

Deal with your unresolved issues

If you have any unresolved issues, you better take care of it. You can learn about your unresolved issues through introspection. When you resolve all of your issues, you eliminate potential emotional minefields. Energy vampires utilize the tactic of surprise attacks. However, when you resolve all of your issues or at least make a mental note of resolving them, you will become grounded and less susceptible to getting attacked by energy vampires. Your unresolved issues can touch upon your friends, family, and even work colleagues.

Stay away from drugs

Drug abuse is one of the pitfalls of being an empath. In the early stages, an empath will have no knowledge of their ability to soak up other peoples' energies. So, they end up mistaking other peoples' negativity as their own. They feel conflicted because they cannot explain the volatile nature of their emotions. Thus, they turn to alcohol to suppress their pain, but alcohol only worsens the problem. Alcohol might seem like a solution, considering that it makes them forget their troubles –

but only for a moment. The energies of other people will still come back, stronger than ever, and it will take even more alcohol to suppress those emotions. It degenerates into a dirty little trap. Don't abuse drugs thinking that they will help drive away your intense emotions. Alcohol won't help you solve that, but even worse is the fact that you will acquire more challenges to overcome, i.e., addiction.

Stay busy

To avoid getting attacked by energy vampires, ensure that you stay focused. You can achieve this by ensuring that you are always pursuing your dreams. Actually, the more time you spend chasing your dreams, the fewer chances energy vampires will have to attack you. However, the more time you waste doing pointless activities or pursuing vain things, the more chances energy vampires have of attacking you. Staying on your purpose doesn't mean that you will no longer get attacked by energy vampires, but it will keep you away from their radar. But remember: an energy vampire can be anybody – even your work colleague.

Stay grounded

A grounded person has a sense of direction. They know what they want and are actively pursuing their goals. A person who is not grounded is indecisive and has no direction. Non-grounded people are very susceptible to the tricks of energy vampires. For instance, if an energy vampire in the form of an old man walked up to an indecisive young woman by the road and promised her heaven in return for sexual favors, the woman might find herself agreeing. This comes from not knowing what you want from life so that you chase shiny things.

Let go of the need to be validated

Most empaths find themselves stuck in a cycle of negativity because of their intense need to fit in and feel validated.

Understand that because you are an empath, you're way different from most people. It is good to fit in and find a tribe that affords you a sense of belonging, but if you don't find people who understand you, then it's fine to stand out. If you don't conform to societal standards, wear your status as a badge of honor, instead of being ashamed. This will make people bend your way and want to accept you, regardless of your weird traits.

Learn to be assertive

One of the best tips for stopping absorbing other peoples' energies is always to speak your mind. Don't be afraid that people will consider you obnoxious or self-entitled. If you suppress your emotions, you will absorb not only other peoples' energy but also become resentful. Being assertive is all about expressing your needs and also respecting the needs of other people.

Shield yourself

Some healers cater to the problem of banishing energy vampires. Some of them administer concoctions, and others encourage the use of energy shields. When protecting yourself through an energy shield, you have to imagine a light surrounding your body so that neither your energy leaves you nor other peoples' energies come into you. The light forms a protective layer around you.

Chapter 12: Coping Strategies for Highly Sensitive People

The following are some strategies that highly sensitive people may utilize to cope with their situations:

Create a routine

As an empath, you're prone to deviate from your plans because you feel different emotions depending on where you are or what time it is. One of the ways you may deal with this problem is by creating a routine. Have a routine that informs your every action. For instance, have a night and morning routine. This way, you won't have trouble figuring out what to do during the night or in the morning. Your routine should be flexible and give room for all the activities that are important for both your physical and spiritual nourishment. When you have a routine, energy vampires will have fewer opportunities to barge into your life and take advantage of you.

Adequate sleep

Getting adequate sleep is not only great for keeping energy vampires away but also improves the quality of your life. Scientists say that you should get at least six hours of sleep every day to function normally. If you get adequate sleep, you will be much grounded. However, if you get poor-quality sleep, you will exhibit nervousness, and you won't be in a position to make the right choices. Sleep helps strengthen your body cells. The more sleep you get, the better your mental and physical body becomes, and it helps in fighting off the attacks of energy vampires.

Improve your self-esteem

If you have low self-esteem, energy vampires are going to be drawn to you as though magnetized. Energy vampires can tell low self-esteem when they see it. Your mannerisms and speech are a dead giveaway to the level of your self-esteem. Learn to exhibit powerful mannerisms and body language so that you can send the message that you have high self-esteem and are not afraid of defending your rights. When you improve your self-esteem, you will not only ward off the energy vampires, but you will also increase the overall quality of your life.

Get a massage

Soaking up the emotions of other people is never a pleasant thing. In fact, when an empath soaks up too much energy from the outside world, it can result in a meltdown. An empath can calm down their powerful emotions by receiving a massage. When an empath harbors a ton of emotions, it can result in clogged body parts too. It would take a massage to erase the clogging and restore the body to its proper working condition. Massages also help one clear the noise from their mind. They restore a sense of calm and help a person have clarity of thought. Having a strong mind is critical in the fight against energy vampires.

Listen to great music

Another great way of reducing the crushing effect of the emotions that you harbor is through music. Music helps relieve bad emotions and promotes a healthy mind. However, you should be careful about the choice of music. Music laced with negative lyrics will infect you with negativity. But music that extols positivity will make you feel positive. In fact, you should listen to music during the times you feel overwhelmed by the emotions of others, and even during times when you're all right. Listening to music will also help you keep your focus on the things that really matter.

Have some alone time

Empaths need to pull away from the crowd, lest they run out of energy. There is nothing wrong in creating some time for yourself. Society might tell you that it is not all right to stay by yourself, but an empath must withdraw from people to recharge their energy. Spending time alone not only helps you recharge your energy levels but also gives you time to reflect on the state of your life. When you take up the habit of secluding yourself to take stock of your life, you get inspired into taking measures that will help you become a better person. You are in a much better position to notice loopholes that need to be sealed, and also it boosts your creative juices.

Improve your diet

Studies have shown that there is a direct relationship between the food that we consume and our state of mind. If we consume unhealthy foods, we are likely to harbor negativity, and if we consume healthy foods, we are likely to feel positive. Unhealthy foods promote weight gain and cause us to have body-image issues, whereas healthy foods help us achieve perfect bodies, and thus boost our confidence. Focus on having a clean diet so that your mind can have enough resources to fight off negativity and protect you from the attacks of energy vampires.

Take breaks

No other group of people understands the importance of taking a break than comedians. Taking a break is not the same as giving up on your dreams. It is just an admission that you are about to run out of energy (or content) and need to take some time off so that you may recharge. Whatever your line of work is, you can benefit from taking a break. This will help you unload all the emotional baggage that you have and look at your life with a fresh perspective. For instance, if you work in the medical field, it can be tiring being witness to the ailing people over a long time. The emotions pile up in your mind, and you can remember the looks of agony on the patients' faces. When you take a break, you can get rid of those emotions so that you may have a clean slate when you come back to work.

Practice mindfulness

Understand that what matters more than anything else is the life you have at present. Yes, the future does matter, but the present matters even more. Learn to bring your senses to the present and savor every moment. When you focus on the present, you take your mind off the anxieties and worries of the future.

Chapter 13: Things that Highly Sensitive People Require

The following are some things that highly sensitive people require to lead quality lives:

Meaningful relationships

Admittedly, no one is an island. An empath will need a partner to feel complete. However, there isn't a very big pool of people that would appeal to an empath. It is not that empaths have impossibly high standards. Empaths can only get along with people who have certain traits and are willing to accept the empath as they are. Sadly, the average person walking on the street is proud and inflexible. It is hard to make them the type of person that would be appreciative of an empath. When an empath meets a partner with whom they can form a meaningful relationship, that's a huge leap forward for the empath in question.

Decompression chamber

When an empath is in a noisy place or subjected to a high-pressure activity, such as a job interview, they can't wait to run into some quiet room and lock themselves away. In a home setting, there should be a chamber which the empath may retreat into whenever they need to kick their energy levels back up. If there aren't resources to create a decompression chamber, the empath might walk out and spend time in the natural world. Empaths have a deep connection with nature.

Conflict management skills

Empaths have such a sensitive side to them that they have a difficult time facing off with another person. Their sensitive nature discourages them from expressing their needs or defending their rights. Thus, during a conflict, an empath is likely to get the short end of the stick. Empaths need to develop their conflict management skills so that other people won't take advantage of them. Conflict management is all about developing the right communication style and knowing what you want. For instance, if an empath is sitting down in their restaurant, and then a drunk veers from the road and crashes their car into the restaurant, the empath should have no qualms about asking the drunk to cater to the repair expenses. If the empath fails to handle this conflict well, the drunk might escape without having to shoulder the responsibility.

Enough time

An empath likes having a lot of time to complete a task. They are not the type that performs under pressure. Empaths tend to have a streak of perfectionism that demands that they slow down their pace to ensure that everything has fallen into place. When you rush an empath, they won't be in a position to deliver high-quality results, and they may even abandon whatever they are doing. The trick is to give the power to the empath. Let them know that they can take the time that they want as long as the results are awesome.

Healthy meals

Food plays a big role in the quality of our lives. If we consume unhealthy food, our lives become terrible, but if we consume healthy foods, our lives become fulfilling. An empath should ensure that they have a balanced diet. A balanced diet consists not only of the important vitamins and minerals but also fresh vegetables and fruits. Empaths should eliminate junk as it would make them susceptible to the attacks of the energy vampire. When you consume junk, you suppress your mental powers, and it becomes easier for a parasite to attach itself onto you and suck the energy off of you.

Minimalism

An empath is not necessarily moved by shiny things. They love simple yet elegant things. Empaths require living in a minimalist arrangement. A minimalist space is the opposite of opulence. They may have the resources to acquire untold luxuries, but they will still opt for the minimalist designs because they appreciate simplicity. For instance, an empath would appreciate being in a house that is furnished with the basic stuff and hasn't gone overboard. Empaths also tend to attach sentimental value to various things. For instance, a piece of clothing or furniture will remind them of a special person, and that piece of furniture or clothing will have more value – in an empath's eyes – than the shiniest thing money can buy.

Considerate people

The average person would have a hard time understanding the empath, but it doesn't mean that they cannot do it. I mean, here's someone who says that they can soak up the energy of whomever they interact with – where do we begin? For the average person, that kind of situation needs a bit more explanation. Empaths have no problem explaining their unique abilities. However, in the same breath, people should be more understanding. They should get along with empaths without imposing rules on them. It will make them feel loved and appreciated regardless of their weird capabilities.

Meaning

The life of an empath needs to have meaning so that they feel they are of service to humanity. It doesn't matter how much money an empath has in their bank account. If their life is not progressing along the path they had envisioned, if they feel that they cannot achieve their goals, then that's a source of tremendous pain. Empaths have a need for identifying their path and sticking to it.

Sensory stimulation

Like everyone else, empaths take a liking to fun and happy moments. It is a great moment of fun when an empath gets a relaxing massage, watches a movie, and indulges in some other fun activity. Empaths love to get stimulated with happiness too. It freshens up their mind and helps them see the fun side of life.

Friends

It is not enough to have people who merely understand you; you need people who are your kindred spirit. Empaths love meeting other empaths and forming close friendships so that they may help one another. Friends help you get grounded and raise your spirits and keep you focused as you chase your goals.

Chapter 14: How to Deal with Difficult People as a Highly Sensitive Person

As a highly sensitive person, you will often come into contact with people who are hard to deal with. The following are tips on how to handle such people:

Always keep your cool

It can be so tempting to lash out when you encounter someone who is not being reasonable. But don't fall into that temptation. The moment you lash out, you lose your power and make the aggressor look big. You should maintain your cool so that you can be in control of the conversation. For instance, if a client proves to be hard to work with, don't yell at them; instead, stay calm and work out a solution. Yelling at people will only trigger them as they fight for their egos. It takes incredible maturity to maintain your calm when someone is obviously looking for a fight. However, in such instances, you should deflect their efforts and, if possible, ask for the intervention of a bigger influence. Aggressors tend to be confounded when their tricks don't seem to excite the reaction they intended.

Mind your own business

You cannot save the world. Some people are purposely difficult as though they want to see who is triggered by their actions. If you realize that someone has a tendency of wanting to test the patience of other people, you should not give them the satisfaction of falling into their trap. Look the other way and continue minding your business. When they realize that you have no interest in their games, they will drop their act. Always mind your business so that you don't get into much trouble in the first place.

Set boundaries

Boundaries are guidelines that you set for other people expressing the permissible way they can behave toward you, and how you will react if the boundaries are crossed. For instance, if you experience friction at work, you may tell your coworkers that you don't appreciate being disturbed once you start working. When you retreat to your desk, they should stay away and wait to engage you once you're free. Having boundaries helps you manage how other people will behave toward you. You should spell out clear terms regarding your boundaries, and if someone trespasses, make sure to mete out punishment.

Learn to see the bigger picture

Sometimes we are so vested in our own interests that we fail to see the big picture. This attitude tends to promote conflict instead of eliminating conflict. For instance, if you think that your parents are not being reasonable, you can potentially raise hell. In as much as you might think that your parents only want to make your life miserable, think of what they want you to have in the future. If you see their grand plans, it is easy to appreciate what they are doing for you at present.

Choose your battles wisely

You need to choose your battles wisely. There are some battles that you stand no chance of winning – and you know it. For instance, if you work for an impossible boss, it can be so tempting to try to fight them. But think of the power that your boss wields. They can terminate you from work. And then you have nowhere to fight from. Always pick the battles that you know you stand a chance of winning. This will save you much heartache and also boost your winning streak.

Separate the person from the issue

It is so easy to fall into the trap of thinking that another person holds a personal grudge against you. However, when you take things personally, you lose the ability to be objective. Always learn to separate the problem from the person. This will allow you to have a fresh perspective on matters. When you take things personally, you can hardly make any progress – since you will only be interested in taking vengeance. Being objective is critical. It will help you articulate the issue you have with another person and how to solve the problem.

Have a sense of humor

The secret to overcoming your hurdles is to meet them with a sense of humor. For instance, if your life partner makes a decision that hurts you, don't recoil away in horror and start calculating how to hurt them back. Instead, reach out to your sense of humor and see the fun side of what your partner has done. Having a sense of humor will help you pull through life's challenges by increasing your creativity. It allows you to have a new perspective on your circumstances.

Ask for help

What would you do if a 300-pound man hurt you? Obviously, you wouldn't attempt to fight back if you're physically weak. But you might press charges against that person. There are systems and people in place to help you get even with the people who have wronged you. Utilize these systems instead of taking matters into your own hands. If your life partner has wronged you, there's no need of becoming violent; just report them to the relevant authorities. Whenever you find yourself pitted against someone who's unreasonable, instead of going through more pain, reach out to someone who can assist you.

Become experienced

There are two ways of viewing your troubles – as a punishment or as a learning experience. If you consider your trouble to be a punishment, you have a victim mentality, and you won't become a better person. However, if you view your trouble as an opportunity to learn, you will become experienced at spotting patterns that lead to trouble with others. The more experienced you are at handling different types of people, the fewer problems you will have considering that you know how to handle various types. Whenever you are in a tight situation, and someone is giving you a difficult time of it, try to learn their pattern.

Chapter 15: Health Tips for Highly Sensitive People

A highly sensitive person is prone to acquiring various illnesses especially the ones that touch upon the nervous system. Whenever you feel off, it is advisable to seek medical attention. The following are some tips to ensure that you're always on top form health-wise:

Balanced diet

The benefits of a balanced diet are countless. If you incorporate in your diet foods that supply all the vital elements, you will become very healthy. Your brain will become powerful thanks to strengthened brain cells, your digestive system will function optimally, and your skin will acquire a healthy glow. A healthy diet also boosts the immune system. Thus, diseases and infections are kept at bay. If you'd like to enjoy the benefits of a balanced diet, you have to make it your lifestyle as opposed to practicing for a while and then abandoning the entire thing. You will notice that having healthy meals will encourage you to prepare meals at home as opposed to eating out, and this habit will save you money.

Eat regularly

Just as it is important to observe a balanced diet, it is just as important to eat regularly. One of the mistakes people make is to consume a huge amount of food in one go. This causes an overload on your intestines and slows down the physiological activities of your body. However, if you space out your meals, you will get the best of both worlds. You will fulfill your body's need for a constant supply of energy. Spacing out your meals also encourages you to have enough food. You're not supposed to undereat or overeat.

Stay hydrated

Staying hydrated is another tremendous hack for optimizing your health. Water helps you increase both your energy levels and brain function. The more hydrated you are, the higher your capacity to function physically. Water is critical in alleviating stomach-related complications too. You should see to it that you consume enough water every day to protect yourself against infections, strengthen your body's physiological activities, and boost the performance of your body cells. According to medical advice, one should drink several glasses of pure water every day, as well as answer to their thirst as soon as it kicks in.

Utilize your support system

The importance of friends cannot be overstated. Many times, you will go through experiences that will demoralize you, but if you have friends to share such experiences with, you will increase your odds of emerging unscathed. Friends are critical for our mental health. Additionally, friends play a vital role in improving our status. If you lose your job, you can depend on your friends for support so that you can land another job. However, if you have no support system, you expose yourself to very many attacks. Ideally, your support system should be people that you have something in common with. For instance, a passion for the economy, sports, or religion.

Wake up early

The earlier you wake up, the more energy you have to face the day, but if you sleep late, you will wake up feeling sluggish. It is always great to wake up early so that you have enough time to prepare for the day. Studies show that early risers have a greater resolve and high mental capacity. Early risers also find it easy to get started on their work and build up momentum. You should get into this habit so that you can boost your energy levels and eliminate laziness. You will make better choices when you're not influenced by laziness.

Detox

Detoxification is merely the process of eliminating toxins from your body. This is done by cleansing the blood in the liver. It is important to cleanse the blood so that body cells may function at the optimum level. The benefits of a detox are numerous. For instance, detox helps in making the digestive system more efficient, helps alleviate constipation, increases the body's ability to absorb nutrients, increases energy levels, improves fertility, lowers the risk of colon cancer, and promotes weight loss.

Health checkups

Empaths tend to worry over many things. In case of a sneeze, the empath may worry that they have come down with a major illness. An empath should get into the habit of conducting health checkups to ascertain that their body is in perfect condition. If you have regular health checkups, it allows you to spot a problem early enough before it blooms into a dangerous complication. Health checkups help you save money in the long run because you are in a position to get rid of an illness at the early stage before it overwhelms your entire body.

Workout

When you get into the habit of exercising regularly, you increase your energy levels and strengthen your immunity. Your body is in a position to fight off infections and ensure optimum health. Studies show that people who exercise regularly are much happier than people who don't exercise at all. Regular exercises will also help you lose weight by combusting the fat in your body. Workouts promote brain health too. Moreover, regular exercises improve your capacity to enjoy sleep. To reap the full benefits of working out, you should create an appropriate schedule, have the right tools, and work with an instructor.

Deep breathing

One clever trick of handling your overwhelming emotions is through taking deep breaths. It is a classic way of refreshing up and improving your health at the same time. For one, deep breathing helps you alleviate stress and anxiety by calming down the noise in your mind. If you are sluggish, you can raise your energy levels by taking deep breaths. Deep breathing also promotes your heart health. Additionally, it helps you get rid of impurities attached to your lungs. There are various ways of carrying out deep breathing exercises, but the critical thing is to find a serene environment.

Chapter 16: How to Avoid Addiction as an Empath

Empaths are very susceptible to drug abuse. Having the ability to soak up other peoples' energies can be disorienting. An empath may turn to drugs as a way to escape their misery. However, drugs don't offer freedom. It is *always* best to seek positive ways of coping with your addiction apart from indulging in drugs. The following are some tips to help you avoid addiction:

Set goals and pursue them

If you are focused on setting and pursuing your goals, you won't have time to indulge in drug abuse. Setting goals indicates that you are an ambitious person and you want to achieve success. It takes discipline and sacrifices to accomplish your goals. If you're really vested in your goals, you will have little free time to relax, let alone indulge in drug usage. Pursuing your goals will make you a focused person. It will also make you less available to people who would influence you into indulging in drug usage. This pursuit calls for a strong sense of self-belief and courage.

Form a support group

An empath is exposed to many troubles that they don't see coming. Getting into drugs may seem harmless, at first, but once you go there, it is hard to escape. To not succumb to the temptation of drugs, empaths must utilize support groups. A support group is made up of members that share a common interest. When each of you looks out for one another, it decreases the chances of anyone deviating. A support group provides a safe haven for the empaths who have already gotten into drugs. The group will support them through their struggle with addiction and see to it that they are back on their feet.

Release pent-up energies

If you have soaked up the energies of other people, it is critical to get rid of them, lest they impede you from having a great life. More often than not, pent-up energies are in the form of negative emotions, and they cause your health to deteriorate. Before you release pent-up energies, you first have to be introspective so that you might see the exact emotions that you have repressed. Once you have figured out the energies that you have repressed, it gets easier to get rid of them.

Don't associate with drug users

You don't want to spend time with drug addicts, lest they infect you with their dishonorable behaviors. As an empath, you are more susceptible to acquiring the traits of another person, and so you want to limit your interactions with people who have negative qualities. However, this doesn't amount to becoming a snob and shunning others. You should ensure that you don't stay close to a drug abuser for long enough to ape their traits. This ability calls for willpower on your part.

Be adventurous

It can be very expensive to sustain an addiction, especially if you're into hard drugs. But think about all the awesome things you would have spent your money on instead of drugs. Whenever you are overwhelmed and feel like trying drugs, remind yourself to channel your money into an adventure instead. For instance, you can embark on traveling on long journeys. Just hop into the bus and travel someplace else. Traveling has a therapeutic effect because it takes you away from the environment that you were wounded. Also, traveling helps you explore the world and come into contact with people from diverse backgrounds.

Take a break

An empath is likely to turn to drugs when they suffer a meltdown. Instead of enduring pain until your breaking point, learn to take short rests. Breaks will allow you to recharge and go back. However, if you don't take breaks, the pressure will be too much, and you may find yourself getting into drugs as a coping strategy. When you take a break, you should use that time to take stock of your life. As an empath, you need to be extremely self-aware so that you can tell apart your energies from those of other people.

Learn to say NO

An empath is a sensitive soul who doesn't want to disappoint anyone. But understand that you cannot please everyone. And if you come across as passive, people will take advantage of you. So, when someone tries to introduce you to drugs, you should have no qualms about saying a big and emphatic NO. This won't cause them to hate or disrespect you; the opposite is true. People will respect you for your ability to defend your beliefs. However, to become comfortable saying NO, you have to practice. Don't say NO just once and then forget about it.

Volunteer in an addiction center

You won't probably understand how addiction ruins lives until you get a close encounter with addiction victims. Instead of taking up a drug, why don't you volunteer in an addiction center? You get a front-seat view of how drug addiction ravages peoples' lives. I bet if you're the type that learns from the mistakes of other people, witnessing drug addicts would discourage you from ever taking drugs. For an empath, being a volunteer would satisfy your intense desire to be altruistic and see that you have a positive contribution to society.

Seek professional help

Never underestimate the efficiency of trained personnel. If you're struggling with obsessive thoughts and are on the verge of getting into drug use, have the courage to seek a counselor. With the help of a professional, you will gain insight into your behavior and the dangers that you subject yourself to by indulging in drug usage. A professional counselor will help you understand your condition even deeper. Seek a counselor who has experience handling empaths that struggle with addiction. If you cooperate with them, you will not only get rid of your addiction problem but also become an even better empath.

Chapter 17: Ways Empaths Love Differently

Falling in love is a great thing if you have an amazing partner. Empaths make the best partners because they are such passionate lovers. The following are some ways empaths love differently:

They are honest

The average relationship tumbles down because of dishonesty. Either one partner or both partners are hiding things from one another, and this causes a tremendous strain on the relationship. When there's dishonesty in a relationship, it becomes difficult to make progress because the partners are not on the same page. However, an empath is as honest as can be. They have nothing to hold back. They love telling it as they see fit and they'd appreciate the same honesty back. Being in a relationship with an empath means that you won't spend days agonizing about where your relationship stands because they are upfront with you.

They are generous

Empaths are natural givers. They are old souls and have had many lives, and it has taught the value of giving. When an empath is in a relationship, they tend to share their resources with their partner unsparingly. The good thing about their generosity is that there are no strings attached. They give for the sake of giving. When an average person gives, they expect something in return, and it can bring friction into the relationship. Perhaps the most important thing that empaths demand of their partners is respect. If respect is lacking, chances are the empath would stop giving and nurse their broken heart.

Their love is intense

There isn't a more passionate lover than an empath. They bare their souls to their lover. It can be quite hard for an empath to fall in love, but once they do, they are intense lovers. Empaths like feeling the sensation of being truly in love. And they seem to believe in true love. Empaths want a relationship to work, and it breaks their heart when their partner doesn't show even half their enthusiasm. Because of their propensity for loving deeply, empaths subject themselves to a high stake of pain. If the relationship were to end, the empath would be far more crushed.

They will give you space

When a partner hogs all the space, the relationship can quickly become boring. Partners ought to take frequent breaks to renew their attraction for each other and take time to build themselves up. An empath will often retreat into solitude to shake off the various energies they have absorbed from other people. Their need for solitude also frees up their partner. Being in a relationship with an empath, you get the best of both worlds – quality time and space. Additionally, empaths will sense when you are not in your best spirits and leave you alone to recover.

Empaths don't project their pain onto their partners

What happens in an average relationship when one partner undergoes a meltdown? The other partner is subjected to immense mental and emotional torture. The suffering partner has valid reasons for being hostile, but still, it's not a good enough reason for making their partner suffer along with them. When an empath is going through a tough time, they tend to distance themselves from their partner so that they may not project their pain onto their partner. This is an incredibly thoughtful thing. When the average person is going through personal stuff, they subject the rest of the world to terrible treatment and assume that it's okay. Although empaths choose to suffer alone, their partners should not ignore them, but take it as an opportunity to lend a helping hand.

They are in tune with partner's feelings

When someone is in a relationship with an empath, the empath will know them too well. The empath has a deep understanding of their partner's feelings. It is almost as though the empath has known them for a lifetime. An empath will know what their partner is feeling by just looking at their face. An empath has an innate ability to detect the feelings of people. This ability enables them to give appropriate responses regarding the feelings of their partners. For instance, if their partner is sad, the empath will know and comfort them or give them space. And if their partner is excited, the empath will still know and play along with that mood.

They are loyal

Empaths don't fall in love at the snap of a finger. They take time. They know that they are intense lovers and they want to be sure that they are making the right decision. However, once they fall in love, they only have eyes for their lover. They cannot play games with their lover by falling in love with other people. Empaths also expect the favor to be returned. They want their partner to be just as committed to them. However, when it doesn't happen, and the empath finds out that their partner is seeing other people, it causes them immense pain. Apart from respect, another important thing that an empath requires is loyalty.

They are intuitive

Empaths have very advanced intuition. They can read into any situation through their hearts. This ability gives them tremendous power when it comes to making important life choices. The empath can make precise judgments. Their intuitive capabilities can be put to use on nearly every aspect of life – socially, economically, and even politically. Intuition is a great tool that helps you create a path that leads into fortune and not destruction.

They are pacifists

A pacifist is someone who is interested in making peace when there are conflicts. When the average person encounters trouble in their relationship, they are not usually willing to eat a humble pie for the sake of the relationship. They are vested in protecting their ego, and that makes them antagonistic. An empath, on the other hand, is all about making peace. They are ready to make compromises for the sake of the relationship.

Chapter 18: Why is it Hard for Empaths to Get into Serious Relationships?

Just like everyone else, empaths want to be in a stable relationship too. However, they find getting into serious relationships a tad difficult. The following are some reasons why empaths have a hard time getting into relationships:

Poor socialization skills

Empaths are not very gifted when it comes to navigating social settings. They are incredibly sensitive to what people say, and they can be hurt by words or actions that were not meant to hurt them. For empaths, mixing with other people is a daunting task, and this affects their capacity to connect with people who can potentially become their significant others. Empaths are sometimes unaware of various social cues. This sends a conflicting message and may make people wary of them. The reason empaths have poor socialization skills is mostly due to their upbringing. If they had started from an earlier age to socialize, they would have acquired the skills and become good at it. But since empaths are not good at socializing yet, it hinders their chance of meeting a person to get into a committed relationship with.

They internalize their partner's issues

An empath is sensitive to the feelings of their partner. If their partner is going through some hardship, the empath will share in the pain. Most people find this ability odd in a partner. Actually, some people would consider it a nuisance. It breaks an empath's heart to know that their concern is not welcome. Their partners stop taking them seriously because they think they are somewhat clingy. Sadly, the empath's ability to feel the pain of their partner deeply is not something that can be wished away.

Attract people who want to be saved, not loved

Empaths are extremely kind. This puts them on the radar of people who like taking advantage. If someone has a problem taking care of their affairs, they might want to attach themselves on an empath and become parasitic. For instance, an empath female is more likely to be approached by a narcissistic man. The narcissist will have wonderful things to say about the woman, making her drop her guard. However, once the woman lets him into her life, his true parasitic nature will come out. He may start borrowing her money for investment purposes and waste her time. The man will make himself look like someone who is in need of help, and the empath is likely to oblige.

People don't understand them

Try explaining to the average person what an empath is like. They will not relate. Empaths have a hard time fitting in society because they appear "out of the norm". Their ability to soak up the energies of other people and perceive them as if they were their own can complicate matters. Empaths would have an easy time getting into relationships if the people they were interested in made some effort to understand them.

The empath is moody

Moody people make terrible partners because you are never quite sure how they will act the next moment. An empath is always processing various emotions, and the nature of their emotions will change depending on their environment. If they are around negative people, empaths will pick up on the negativity and potentially display a foul mood. This can make their potential partners wary of them. Empaths have a hard time because, in as much as they are moody, they hate having to subject their partners to horrible treatment. They may start to hide whenever they are moody.

Too sincere

Is it possible that sincerity can hold you back from getting into a relationship? Certainly! Not that being sincere is a bad thing. But some people prefer being lied to for the purpose of preserving their egos. For instance, if an empath goes out to a party with someone with a potential to become their life partner, and then that person behaves in a manner that the empath thinks is obnoxious, the empath will tell them exactly what they think. If the empath had wanted to massage their partner's ego, they should lie. But this ability of theirs to be sincere kind of antagonizes their partner.

Attitude problem

It's no secret that empaths are incredibly sensitive. They tend to vet the words and actions of other people as if trying to read into the hidden message. This habit causes them to be hurt by things that don't hurt well-adjusted people. Empaths may sometimes think that the world is against them. Ultimately, their sensitive nature ruins their attitude. Anyone expressing interest in an empath might go through a minefield, thanks to their tendency of taking things personally. In a relationship, there won't be a shortage of faults, but partners must have huge hearts, not small hearts that take things personally.

Hates conflict

Empaths tend to avoid conflict as ardently as they can. When they realize that a conversation is headed toward conflict, they will back off. And if threats are issued, an empath will get scared. Empaths would rather not solve a problem than endure the pain of fighting for what they believe in. This habit tends to send people away. People know that a good relationship partner must be willing and ready to handle conflict for the good of both partners.

Seem aloof

The tendency of an empath to withdraw from human interaction may pass off as aloofness. And looking in from the outside, the empath in question might seem like an arrogant person. Those who have no idea what's going on will consider the empath to be emotionally distant. Such a conclusion can harm the social standing of the empath and lower the number of people who are interested in them. At the end of the day, human beings are social creatures, and we tend to disassociate from people who cannot seem to fit in. If everyone understood why empaths pull away, they wouldn't shun them.

Chapter 19: Why Empaths and Narcissists are Attracted to Each Other and the Stages of their Relationship

Although it is common for empaths to fall for narcissists, they never do so with the sole intention of saving them as many people assume. Narcissists are skilled at setting traps for sensitive individuals, and more often than not, they manage to trap the empath. The personalities of the two are diametrically opposite. And for some reason, their attraction tends to be impassioned, up until the empath learns the true colors of the narcissist. Then the relationship goes up in flames. The following are stages that a relationship between an empath and a narcissist must go through:

1. The narcissist targets an empath and closes in on them. They project themselves as a dynamic person with a unique personality that awes the empath. The empath hesitates, wanting to eliminate all doubt. Then the empath swallows hook, line, and sinker, and falls

head over heels in love with the narcissist. The initial phase of their love is intense and passion-filled.

2. The narcissist passes themselves as a faultless person full of love. The empath buys this and continues to be loyal to the narcissist. They are thinking that they have found someone special and this is a match made in heaven. The empath starts feeling a deep bond connecting them to the narcissist.

3. The empath notices that though the narcissist is interested in the relationship, it is as if they want the empath to give their time and money, whereas the narcissist holds all the power in the relationship. Their love for power flashes in little, eyebrow-raising ways. However, the narcissist reassures the empath that all is right by putting on a fake persona.

4. The narcissist will launch their first attack on the empath. It may be an accusation of not behaving properly or some other problem the narcissist has with the empath. Their attacks are aimed at shifting the power to them and discourage the empath from wanting to be their equal.

5. The empath starts to feel weary and disillusioned. They have begun to suffer under the hands of the narcissist. On the one hand, the narcissist flashes their meanness, and on the other hand, they are sweet and fun to be around. They hurt the empath and then become good people and it confuses the empath.

6. The abuse that the narcissist metes out on the empath is merely emotional. They want to arrest the soul of the empath. The goal of the narcissist is to make the empath give up their power and accept that they are inferior to the narcissist. They succeed.

7. The empath now fully believes that the narcissist is the one in control and they believe that the narcissist will make decisions that will benefit them both. The empath seems to think that love and suffering go together. They are ready to suffer through discomfort just to make the narcissist happy.

8. The narcissist starts portraying themselves as the victim of circumstances. They will start to say that they have been hurt in the past by lovers and even parents. This is their plan for getting the sympathy of the empath. They want to win the trust of the empath.

9. Whatever sob story the narcissist has told the empath will be greeted with suspicion by the empath, but their sensitive side cannot rubbish whatever they have been told. Narcissists want to pass themselves off as victims. It gives them power. And just as they planned, the empath starts feeling sorry for them and believes that the narcissist is in need of their help.

10. The narcissist asks for a favor from the empath. It is normally a small favor. The empath obliges. Then what follows is a flurry of requests for more favors. The narcissist is a parasite and they want to use every resource that the empath owns. Whether it is time or money, narcissists will see to it that their empaths give up a significant portion of their resources. The work of the empath is to give. They ought to trust the narcissist will put the resources to good use.

11. The empath loses them totally into the relationship. The narcissist is the "rock star" of the relationship and they are in charge of making key decisions and determining where the relationship is headed. The empath would like to have a contribution, but the narcissist hogs all the space.

12. Then the empath realizes that their wishes are not being respected and that they have lost their identity trying to please the narcissist. For once, the empath speaks up, wanting to know why they are not treated as though they matter in the relationship.

13. The narcissist does not like the new attitude of the empath. They try to put them back in their place by cementing their status as the holder of power in the relationship. This action is aimed at making the empath submit to the narcissist. The narcissist wants the empath to realize that they are in control for the good of both.

14. The empath is obviously confused. They have awakened to how gross their partner is by this time. Obviously, they won't back down, but they will increase their effort to demand fair treatment. Empaths still want to work on the relationship instead of letting it go to the dogs. They want the narcissist to be reasonable.

15. The narcissist doesn't make any adjustments. Everything stays as bleak as the empath has come to observe. The empath is filled with tremendous pain as they awaken to the reality that they fell in love with a fake image. The empath becomes deeply sorrowful when they realize what this means for their relationship. But still, they want to salvage the relationship, if only the narcissist would cooperate.

16. The narcissist obviously is unrepentant and they even double down on their ruthlessness. Finally, the empath realizes that the narcissist doesn't deserve their affection. They break off the relationship and enter a phase of immense grief. However, when the pain goes away, they will move on, never to think back to the narcissist.

Chapter 20: Is Your Child an Empath? Tips for Raising Them

If your child is an empath, you must have realized that they have special qualities. Some of the traits they may exhibit include being intuitive, having a deep connection with animals, and being extremely sensitive. You want to bring them up in a way that will encourage their condition. The following are tips for raising an empath child:

- **Nothing is wrong with them**: An empath child might think that something is wrong with them when they don't seem to fit in with the rest, but it is your responsibility as a parent to let them know that they are just fine. Let your child know that they don't need to be fixed. They are fine.
- **Make the environment peaceful**: Empaths are extremely sensitive to noise. They cannot function in an environment that is chaotic. You have to ensure that your child grows up in a tranquil setting. If they grow up in a disorganized area, they will get distracted and lose focus.
- **Watch their associations**: Empath children are extremely impressionable. They are sensitive to the needs of other

children. They have a deep desire to fit in. So, they will try to eagerly associate with many kids, some of whom might not be the best. Watch the kids that your child wants to associate with and study their behaviors. If they are bad-mannered kids, encourage your child to stop associating with them, lest they pick up their manners.
- **Never mock your child**: If your child is very sensitive to people's words or actions, it can be tempting to rebuke them. However, mocking them wouldn't make them develop a tough skin; instead, you would make the child resent you for not understanding them. As the parent, you want to be your child's best ally, and you must provide guidance without mocking them.
- **Use different disciplinary measures**: You must not punish an empath child as you would the average kid. You must not subject them to pain and suffering. An empath child is very obedient, and they are capable of correcting their ways if you guide them patiently. If you use pain, they might take it personally and resent you for that.
- **Quality rest**: The importance of rest cannot be overstated. Soaking up other people's energies can be extremely tiring. You must provide a great environment for your child to have quality sleep. This will play a big role in the energy levels of your child. The more sleep they get, the bouncier they act.
- **Encourage them to talk**: An empath child is likely going to be quiet. However, beneath their calm exterior, there is a tsunami of emotions. Encourage your child to talk out their feelings so that they won't slip into depression. This is a major way of showing that you care about their wellbeing.
- **Be an emotion coach**: After encouraging them to talk out their feelings, it is on you to make them understand their emotions. Teach them how their emotions contribute to the person that they end up becoming. But more importantly, get them to be aware of their ability to soak up other people's emotions and pass them off as their own.

- **Improve their collaboration skills**: Since an empath child will have a hard time fitting in, they might isolate themselves from others, and this will affect their capacity to perform within a team. Collaboration is critical for success. Involve them in some of your activities and encourage them to involve other kids too.
- **Praise them**: Kids are desperate to win the approval of their parents. When they do something great, for instance, when they score their target grade, that's a perfect opportunity to reward their effort. Praise them and reward them for their achievements. This will give them the drive to carry on accomplishing big things.
- **Teach them how to establish boundaries**: Your empath child is going to be the kindest among other kids. This can make them susceptible to narcissistic parasites. Teach them that their kindness should have limits. It's no longer kindness if they suffer from it. Teach them to first satisfy their needs before lending a helping hand to others.
- **Develop their creativity and imagination**: An empath child is going to have a fertile imagination. Teach them how to get the most out of their imagination. It will help them overcome their problems. You can improve their creativity by providing reading materials appropriate for their age. The more they read, the more they stretch the limits of their creativity.
- **Improve their communication skills**: If you're not proactive about this, your child might end up having a speech impediment. To eliminate the chances of this ever happening, you have to teach your child how to express themselves. This is a vital skill that will be extremely critical in their adult life.
- **Teach them how to handle pressure**: An empath child is going to be subjected to immense pressure from peers. The peer group of the empath child will always notice that they are quirky. They will pressure them to become like the rest.

In those times, the empath child must not buckle but continue being themselves.
- **Exercise**: You should begin training your child physically from an early age. Regular exercises for your child will improve their physical and emotional health. Exercising will also strengthen their character and integrity. Thus, they will be in a position to make impactful decisions, instead of being weak and indecisive.
- **The value of gratefulness**: An empath child is going to be grateful for everything that they have – or are given. But still, you have to cement this ideal so that it becomes a lifelong value of theirs. Make your child understand that they must be grateful no matter what.

Chapter 21: Best Career Choices for Empaths

The beauty of life is that there is so much diversity. When it comes to jobs, particular personalities go with different jobs. We cannot all do the same job for the simple reason that we don't share a single personality type. Human beings are varied. For instance, an extrovert could do very well as a salesperson, but an empath wouldn't perform well in the same job. The following are some career fields that empaths thrive in:

Nurse

Caring for others comes naturally to empaths. An empath would thrive in the nursing field where they would have to take care of sick people. Empaths get a big relief out of making a big impact in the world that they live in, and nursing a sick person back to health would be incredibly helpful. You can take up jobs in hospitals, nursing homes, or even open your private practice.

Psychologist

Mental illness has become such a great problem, especially in the modern world and there are not enough psychologists to handle the situation. Empaths would make perfect psychologists since they love to both help people get back on their feet and gain a deeper understanding of the workings of the brain.

Writer

Empaths tend to experience intense emotions. And they also have a very introspective side to them. These are perfect ingredients for a great writer. Pursuing a career in the writing industry would be incredibly satisfying considering that they won't have to endure the noise and distractions from the outside world. They can create their own small world.

Accountants

Considering that empaths have a hard time mixing with people and that they struggle with soaking up other people's energies, a career as an accountant is in order. They would be in the background crunching the figures. And human contact would be restricted to when they are reporting to their bosses or liaising with co-workers.

Veterinarian

Empaths not only care for human beings; their love extends to animals. They want to ensure that animals are relieved of pain too. If they take up work as a veterinarian, they will be instrumental in improving the lives of animals around the world. Recent studies have indicated that animals have feelings too.

Artist

Another line of work that welcomes an empath's intense feelings and unique perspectives is the arts. An empath can tap into their wealth of emotions to create art that moves people. Thanks to the various online platforms that cater to selling art, they would have an easy time reaching their target audience and creating a fan base.

Life coach

Empaths are deeply introspective. This quality of theirs has led them to gain a very deep insight into life. An empath may choose to become a life coach to enlighten other people. People will flock to the empath to drink from their fountain of wisdom. As a life coach, they may open an office or even perform it through the internet.

Teacher

Banking on their immense desire to offer guidance to impressionable minds, an empath would do extremely well as a teacher. Empaths are patient, and students would take an instant liking to them, especially because they would feel understood. Empaths take pleasure in seeing that they played a role in transforming the life of an individual.

Non-profit organization worker

The truth of the matter is that millions of people are hurting around the world. Some organizations help improve the situation of these people. These organizations are in need of workers who aren't money-minded. An empath cares about the plight of the afflicted and is not swayed by money, and thus would make a very good candidate for this type of job.

Website and graphic designer

The traditional way of performing business is experiencing a major shift. People are turning to the internet to grow their business. An empath would take advantage of this development by setting up their own website design and graphic design agencies. Many entrepreneurs want to work with website and graphic designers to create a great website for their business.

Virtual assistants

Many people have shifted to doing businesses online. The e-commerce industry in America alone is worth hundreds of billions. There are stressed executives who need help in the form of virtual assistants. You would lighten their burden by providing the service of virtual assistance. This would involve things like reminding them of important schedules, ensuring company documents are securely stored, among other things.

Botanist

Empaths find themselves connected to plants too. They can almost communicate with a plant just by picking up its vibrations. Becoming a botanist is suitable because they now have a chance to understand the science of plant life. This career would satisfy their need to understand how plants come into being and produce the food that we consume.

Landscape design

Empaths are creative people. They would surely succeed in a career in landscape design. This career calls for an understanding of landscape architecture and garden design. But empaths would thrive because of their creativity and intuition. Clients would have a blast working with them because they would seem to get the client very fast and produce the exact designs that the clients had wanted.

Real estate broker

Empaths would thrive in this line of work because real estate brokerage is an extremely peaceable affair. Most of their time would be consumed with scouting locations and trying to find leads. The business doesn't involve too many people. Also, it would relieve empaths to see that they had helped someone find a comfortable place to live.

Digital Marketer

In the age of the internet, starting a marketing agency is the easiest thing ever. There are hundreds of millions of online shoppers willing to spend money. As a digital marketer, your work is to create the perfect product and sell it to your online clientele. Empaths would thrive in this line of work, especially since they can utilize automation tools and tone down human contact.

Chapter 22: Signs You're an Intuitive Empath – Not Just an Empath

An intuitive empath has a profound capacity of intuiting the thoughts and actions of people. This ability has been with them ever since they were small. An intuitive empath is a special kind of empath, and the following traits are distinct to them:

Vivid dreams

An intuitive empath experiences vivid dreams. These dreams are never lost on an empath. This capability of theirs started when they were small kids and has stuck with them into adulthood. Intuitive empaths are very much in love with the dream world and can't seem to wait for the night so that they can jump into another dream. Considering that dreams bypass the ego, they are usually very powerful mediums of providing intuitive information. Dreams bring about guidance on matters of spirituality and healing, as well as overcoming terrible emotions. Dream elements may be symbolic too. However, an intuitive empath is equipped to decode the hidden meaning of every character that appears in their dreams. The dream of an empath is more often than not message-laden. Maybe it's a revelation or a healing message. Intuitive empaths utilize these dreams in providing solutions for what ails them or the people that they care about.

Some intuitive empaths have spirit guides whom they talk to within the dream world. The spirit guide can take the shape of an animal, person, angel, or even voice, but their presence is unmistakable. Spirit guides normally give you the wisdom of overcoming your life challenges, actualizing your goals, and living more creatively and peaceably. Spirit guides have no malicious intent and are actually interested in improving the life of the intuitive empath along with their friends.

During dreams, an intuitive empath has the capability of moving from the present world and touring through the dream-verse. This is called an out-of-body experience. It is surreal. An empath who is used to this kind of experience can find themselves missing sleeping, as they cannot wait to go on another trip into the worlds beyond our thin veil of reality.

The dream-history of intuitive empaths is extensive and to ensure that none of that is lost, you have to record it. When you wake up, write down the details of your dream in a journal. Then meditate on the meaning of those dreams during the rest of the day. Get into the habit of asking yourself significant questions before you go to bed. This way, you will encourage your spirit guides to give you an answer through a dream.

Mystic capabilities

Another sure sign of an intuitive empath is their mystic powers. An intuitive empath is the type of person to take a casual glance at someone and read their minds like a textbook. They know what your hidden thoughts are, what you are about to do, and what you truly think about various things.

An intuitive empath is the sort of person that will think to themselves, "My mom has gone two days without speaking to me," and just as they contemplate that absurdity, their phone will start buzzing and guess who's calling? Momma!

An intuitive empath is the sort of person who will be sitting around and suddenly think, "My child is sick," and then they will learn later that their child is sick.

An intuitive empath faces the challenge of detecting whether a certain thought that they have is independent or a projection of their emotions and struggles. Chances of a thought being accurate are high when that thought appears independently, as opposed to it being an extension of an intuitive empath's emotional state.

It is absolutely necessary for an intuitive empath to develop a profound sense of self-awareness. Information received when you're in a neutral or compassionate state is far more accurate than messages received when you are emotionally charged. However, if an intuitive empath has a profound understanding of self, they will hardly project their fears, worries, or insecurities onto other people.

As an intuitive empath, it is absolutely necessary for you to stay grounded. The vibrations you pick up off of other people shouldn't complicate your life. On the contrary, they should deepen your compassion and understanding for others. The ability to read into people's hidden thoughts is rare. At the back of your mind, you should know that you're extremely fortunate.

Connected to mother earth

Intuitive empaths are very much connected to mother earth. They can perceive various natural bodies – sensually and energetically. If it's the thunder, they can perceive its power rattling through their body, and if it's the moon, they can perceive its beauty welling up inside them.

An intuitive empath seems to be attuned to the energy status of the earth. They are happy when mother earth is well taken care of, and sad when mother earth acts with fury. If an intuitive empath lives near the ocean and the waters are calm, the empath will feel nourished and happy. However, if the waters become violent, the initial happiness escapes them, and in its place, comes depression.

The intuitive empath is such unicorn, for they are happy when the earth is in great condition, and sad when the earth suffers any harm. For this reason, the empath must take an active role in ensuring that the earth is well taken care of. The intuitive empath must also spend time in the natural world to experience the state of oneness.

Foreknowledge of events

If you're an intuitive empath, you find yourself often telling people, "Didn't I tell you?" This is because you seem to have prior knowledge of things. Either you get visions about the future when you're awake, or you dream about future events, but in both cases, the visions come to pass. This ability is not restricted to your life alone. You may very well predict the future events of other people's lives. You can see what their relationships, careers, and other statuses will be like.

Being an intuitive empath is an immense gift that one should be proud of and take full advantage of to have a fulfilling life.

Chapter 23: How to Remain in Balance with your Emotions

In the face of challenges or change, the emotions of an empath are likely to oscillate between extremes. Their internal atmosphere is chaotic. However, to maintain a healthy body and mind, an empath is supposed to attain emotional balance. The following are some tips to help you remain in balance with your emotions:

Forgive yourself

A quirky trait that nearly all empaths share is their tendency of being too hard on themselves. If they set a goal and fail to achieve it, that is enough to throw them into a state of untold misery. They are too hard on themselves, and they barely know it. It encourages negativity in their life – since they clearly have a scarcity mindset. As an empath, you should learn to let go of your failures, but this doesn't mean that you should become complacent. Re-strategize, set new goals, and have a go at it.

Practice mindful meditation

Mindful meditation is the practice of living in the moment. If you are caught in a cycle of worry for the unknown, there's no better way of relieving yourself of the worry than practicing mindful meditation. You have to focus your energy on clearing the noise from your mind and appreciating the moment that you're in right now.

Deep breathing exercises

The effectiveness of deep breathing exercises in letting go stress and tension cannot be overstated. You have to find a serene environment and assume an erect posture, and then start taking deep breaths in and out. Focus on eliminating the negativity and the stress of life as you inhale and exhale.

Workout

Get into the habit of working out on a daily basis. This will improve your emotional health and make you less susceptible to low moods. Physical exercises will help you acquire an enviable body and make you confident about yourself. When you're feeling confident, you're more likely to experience happy thoughts.

Accept what you're feeling

To pull yourself out of bad emotions, you must first be honest about what you really feel. Though it may bruise your ego to admit that you're struggling with bad emotions, when you are sincere about your feelings, you're in a much better position to overcome those bad emotions than if you hadn't been honest with yourself.

Don't abuse drugs

Some people find solace in drugs when they experience emotional turbulence. Don't take that route. Although drugs might seem like a great solution, the effect is short-lived. You will have to consume more and more drugs to fight away the pain but end up as an addict. You better fight your bad emotions when you're sober. It is not an easy thing, but it is a better alternative.

Drop your expectations

Having lofty expectations can be dangerous when you fail to live up to them. You are likely to become depressed and struggle with obsessive thoughts. You should learn to lower or drop your expectations altogether. When you don't have lofty expectations, it doesn't mean that you should stop working hard. It means that you're focused, yes, but you want the universe to surprise you.

Be grateful

It is so easy to feel like a victim under the weight of bad emotions. However, pause for a moment. Think about what you already have. If you are a grateful person, you are less likely to experience bad emotions since you have an abundance mindset. But if you're an ungrateful person, you will always want more.

Watch your diet

Studies show that there is a big correlation between poor diet and mental health issues like depression and obsessive thoughts. Stop eating junk food and start preparing healthy meals. When you adopt a healthy diet, you will improve both your emotional and physical wellbeing. Additionally, a healthy diet will save you money.

Quality sleep

The more quality sleep you get, the better your mental health will become. Ensure you sleep for at least six hours every night. When you have quality sleep, you will have more energy to face the day, and more importantly, your brain will function at the optimum level. You are less likely to get into situations that will mess up your mood. However, if you're a poor sleeper, you are likely to become irritable and more inclined into having bad emotions.

Embrace other people

Stop holding grudges against other people. It doesn't necessarily mean you have forgiven them. However, understand that when you hold grudges, you attract negative energy into your life. Negative energy breeds stress and anxieties. It won't serve you. But if you let go of the grudges, you relieve yourself of the negative energy and position yourself for happiness.

Music

When you're experiencing a tsunami of emotions inside of you, calm yourself down by listening to soothing music. With the right music, you can fight away violent emotions and give room to peace. Studies show that music has a therapeutic effect. Instead of just listening to the music and letting the emotions play out within your mind, you could also sing along, and it will speed up the healing process.

Spend time with friends

Your friends don't exist for the sunshine alone. They should be there for you when it's cloudy and rainy too. When you're down and are struggling with bad emotions, reach out to your friends, and they will help you pull through. If you have cultivated a close relationship with your friends, you may share with them what ails you. However, you have to have close ties with them before you make yourself vulnerable because you could end up looking like a fool.

Become more self-aware

The more you experience different emotions, the more you should heighten your self-awareness. Take it as an opportunity to learn about your true character, feelings, desires, and motives. When you have great self-awareness, you are in a position to keep your emotions balanced.

Chapter 24: Signs You Have Spiritual Healing Capabilities

In the westernized societies, if a person comes down with an illness, a physician is the answer. Modern medicine is useful, yes, but there's even a more potent curative technique known as spiritual healing. This practice is relatively new and hasn't gained wide acceptance yet, but its practitioners know that it works. Spiritual healing is not concerned about alleviating a single disease but restoring wholesome health to an individual. Spiritual healers have known of their potential since they were little. Empaths tend to have an inherent capacity to become spiritual healers. The following are some signs that indicate you have the potential of becoming a spiritual healer:

You almost never get sick

You seem to radiate an energy that keeps you from falling ill. You don't remember ever going to the hospital to receive drugs or an injection. You have always had perfect health. Although you live a normal life like everybody else, you seem not to be affected by the disease-causing germs that affect other people.

You have an odd ability to perceive patterns

It has always seemed that you can unravel a pattern to most things that happen in your life or other people's lives. Ever since you were little, these patterns have just been obvious to you, and other people consider you weird for being able to do that.

You feel connected to animals

You have never understood people who treat animals cruelly. You have such a special bond with animals, and it is almost as though you can communicate with them. You have kept various pets ever since you were little and particularly keep cats or dogs as pets.

You attract children

It is almost as though children are magnetized toward you. It doesn't matter whether the children are not familiar with you, they will still come running and crash into you. Children are very excited around you. And they seem to hang on your every word. They have elevated you into a figure of authority.

You avoid crowds

Crowded areas like shopping malls and nightclubs seem to give you a mini heart attack. The noise produced by all those people sucks the peace out of you. Being surrounded by many people tends to drain your energy. This causes you to actively avoid being caught up in crowds.

You can sense weather change

You tend to instinctively know how the day's weather will pan out. It could be raining now, and your guts tell you that there will be sunshine some other time, and true, the sun shines later. Being sensitive to weather patterns is a rare gift, and if you possess it, you are definitely an energy healer.

People flock to you for help

People trust you for answers. People you barely know often come up to you and 'pour their hearts out'. They seem to think that you have their answers. They ask for advice about dealing with life's frustrations. And just as they hoped, you play that role perfectly well.

You're a very good listener

You have realized that listening is one of your strong traits. People can go on and on without giving you a chance to talk, and you're in the least bit bothered. This ability of yours allows you to be patient enough to let people reveal as much as they can about themselves.

Your hobbies are worlds apart from your peers' hobbies

Perhaps your peers are into playing Ping-Pong, beach partying, or even sports. However, you have zero interest in mainstream hobbies. Your hobbies include things like yoga or reading novels. Your interest in non-mainstream hobbies has made you less visible amongst your peers.

Your dreams come true

Everything that you ever saw in your dreams came to pass. Various elements in your dreams might be symbolic, but you will still have the insight of getting the message. This ability has bestowed on you precognitive powers. You seem to know what the future holds.

You have endured a traumatic event

Maybe you had a sad childhood, and it scarred you for life. The trauma was critical in awakening your spiritual healing capability though. As you have matured, you have consigned the trauma in your past and are thriving at present. But from time to time, the memories appear in the back of your head.

You don't feel a sense of belonging

You have gone to many places and done many things, but you have never quite felt home. You feel like an alien from another planet. You haven't quite met someone that you could call a kindred spirit. Yes, the basic decency is there, but you cannot connect with other people at a primal level. At the start, it used to bother you, but not anymore.

Electromagnetic hypersensitivity

This has made you feel very weird about yourself. When you are around some object radiating electromagnetic signals, you tend to affect its normal functioning. For instance, you might walk into a room and the lights blink, or you may touch a radio, and it suddenly dies down.

You always attract people who need to be saved

Looking back at all the people who came into your life, you are startled to realize that they needed something from you. They needed to be saved. And you did a great job of saving them – or at least tried to.

You have witnessed numerous mystical activities

Deep inside you know that there's more to life than we presently know. You have on various occasions experienced supernatural events that left you baffled. Maybe you were asleep and felt a weird presence in your room, or maybe you have actually seen an entity that can be described as otherworldly. You just know that there is a lot of mystical stuff out there that we haven't figured out yet.

Chapter 25: How to Strengthen Your Mental Body

This is the part of you that comprises thoughts and consciousness. To achieve wholesome health, you have to ensure that your mental body is in proper working condition. Follow the tips below to ensure your mental body becomes stronger:

- **Establish goals**: When you establish a goal, you encourage your mind to help you achieve your desires. A goal must not be handled as a mere wish. You must spell out the exact thing that you want to achieve and impose a time limit. But your goals should be reachable. If you're grounded, you can understand the difference between being ambitious and delusional.
- **Enhance your environment**: Every day, we are subjected to numerous decisions. If our resolve is weak, we can easily succumb to poor decisions. However, we should encourage ourselves to make the right decisions by setting the appropriate environment. For instance, if your purpose is to work out in the evening, put your training shoes in an open area so that when you come back, you will see your shoes

and the thought will kick in. If you want to eat healthily, get rid of junk so that you won't be tempted.
- **Ditch the shortcuts**: If you like taking shortcuts, you will end up nowhere. All good things take effort. The last thing you want is to familiarize your mind with the toxic habit of taking shortcuts. If you're training, ensure that you complete the reps and don't cheat yourself. Staying true to yourself not only helps you achieve your goals but also improves your integrity.
- **Embrace discomfort**: When you become too complacent, you will gradually lose your resolve and end up falling short of your goals. You don't want that to happen. Embrace being uncomfortable. This spirit will see you fight for your dreams. Teach your mind some resilience. This way, you will go against all the odds and achieve what you want.
- **Address your negative thoughts**: As long as there's negativity in your mind, you will hardly ever make progress. As an empath, negativity stifles both your psychic abilities and creativity. It is not possible to wipe out all the negative energy that resides in you, but you should see to it that your negativity is at least lowered.
- **Challenge yourself**: It is through persevering through challenges that we become better than we previously had been. If you're not challenging yourself, then you won't grow. When you condition your mind to expect challenges, you tend to be in the right headspace for performing greatly. However, when you take the easiest path available, you lose both your focus and your fighting spirit.
- **Prove people wrong**: If someone tells you that you can't do something, take it as an encouragement to do it and prove them wrong. As an empath, you will encounter many people who will underrate you, but you must never give them the satisfaction of letting them win. When you prove people wrong, it makes you feel great and also boosts your self-esteem tremendously.

- **Read books**: The more books you read, the more knowledgeable you will become on a number of issues. Knowledge is power. And it really helps to have a developed brain. Studies have found that reading causes the brain cells to increase. This phenomenon is known as neuroplasticity, whereby new brain cells are formed to store new information.
- **Improve your diet**: If you would like to have a well-functioning mental body, you have to clean your diet. Throw out the junk. Start eating healthy foods that comprise all the vital elements. Eat fruits and vegetables too. A great diet is not only beneficial for the mind but also the body as a whole. And don't make a healthy meal once and then forget about it – no! You have to make healthy meals a part of your lifestyle.
- **Exercise**: The importance of working out cannot be overstated. Exercises are great for the health of both the mind and body. The awesome part is that you don't need sophisticated tools to get started. All you need is some space, basic equipment (sometimes nothing at all) and you're good to go. To reap the full benefits, you have to make exercises a part of your lifestyle as opposed to doing it only once.
- **Sleep**: Your mind will relax when you're asleep. The more quality sleep you get, the more your mind becomes refreshed. When your mind is refreshed, you get to have tremendous self-motivation throughout the day, and you are in a position to execute your roles much better. Quality sleep will help raise your vibrations too.
- **Limit the time spent watching TV**: The main purpose of TV is not to entertain you; it's to make money off of you. There's too much content on the television that is both inappropriate and misleading. If you subject yourself to this content, you will become subliminally programmed. So, you have to avoid TV and look for an alternative form of entertainment. Stay away from TV so that you don't get mind

programmed, and more importantly, you can make better use of your time.
- **Break the mold**: If your mind has gotten used to only one way of doing things, you should break the pattern so that your brain might activate the other side, as well as access both hemispheres. Change the way you do things.
- **Reflect**: Don't be so lost in the doing part of it that you forget to live. And there's no better way to live than through reflection. When you stop to look back on your progress, you get to appreciate your contribution, and at the same time, you encourage yourself to become even better.
- **Meet smart people**: This is another incredible way of improving your mind. They say iron sharpens iron. Meet new, intelligent people and get to learn from them.

Chapter 26: What is a Psychic Empath and How to Tell if You're One?

The term empath covers a broad range of people with empathic abilities. A psychic empath has the rare gift of tuning in to the hidden feelings of other people. Psychic empaths are born with this gift, but it only begins to manifest after their childhood. As kids, psychic empaths tend to be shy and sensitive, and their peers tend to treat them with suspicion. If they receive no help, chances are they will have a tumultuous young adult life with the reputation of being social misfits. The following are some traits that psychic empaths exhibit:

Telepathic

Psychic empaths can transmit thought patterns from their minds to another person. Also, they can know the thoughts of other people no matter the distance between them. For instance, a psychic empath will instinctually know when either of their parents is sad or depressed, as they can share in the sadness deep within. A psychic empath could be eating ice cream one moment, and the next moment they sense something is wrong, and when they contact someone about whatever they have thought, it is normally the case.

They have good luck

A psychic empath seems to be followed by good luck. They not only bring luck on themselves but also on other people. For instance, if a psychic empath meets with someone and exchanges greetings, that person will proceed to run into good luck throughout the day. If a psychic empath gives someone some money, chances are the person will run into more good fortune for the better part of that day or week.

They hate conflict

The easiest way to make a psychic empath run away from you is to confront them or issue a threat. They love making peace – not warring. They are extremely turned off by the idea of having to fight as a way of righting a wrong.

High sensory stimulation

The sensory nerves of a psychic empath are very active. For this reason, they tend to react to stimuli much quicker than the average person. A psychic empath can get overwhelmed too easily. For this reason, they tend to avoid places with too much noise or too much light – basically anything on the extreme end. Psychic empaths are also good at detecting sensations that would be lost on the average person. They can detect subtlest things about a place or person.

Their instincts about people are on the money

Psychic empaths seem to know by gut what someone is like. For this reason, if you're a bad person, you won't catch a psychic empath entirely off guard. They will know that you're a bad influence but somehow still give you the benefit of the doubt, and after you reveal your true colors, it will dawn on them that their first instincts were accurate.

They have imaginary friends

A psychic empath is in contact with the spiritual world. They have even made friends with entities in the spiritual realm otherwise known as spirit guides. The spirit guides act as protectors for the psychic empath and reveal secrets and insights to them. Strangely enough, the psychic empath derives more satisfaction from interacting with the spirit guides than they ever would from interacting with regular people.

They appear lonely

To the average observer, a psychic empath can seem to be the loneliest person for they are always alone. However, strangely enough, psychic empaths hardly ever seem needy or emotionally unstable. They may lack human contact, but that doesn't automatically mean that they are lonely. They tend to have very active imaginations. The worlds that they have created in their minds are extremely fun-filled. But then again, there is a percentage of psychic empaths that crave human contact and are actually lonely.

They had a past life

Psychic empaths are old souls who have existed someplace else before. Oddly enough, they seem to have a faint recall of their past lives. A psychic empath will think back to their past life, and though the memory is not vivid, they have a somewhat basic understanding of what life was like in that world.

Communicate with animals

A psychic empath seems to have the uncanny ability to communicate with animals. Maybe they will establish eye contact or touch the animal, and then the information starts flowing. Animals are completely at ease around psychic empaths. In extreme cases, a psychic empath can cause an animal to become animated.

Loving and compassionate

Psychic empaths don't stay away from people because they think they are superior to them; they stay away because people overwhelm them. This doesn't mean that psychic empaths are incapable of expressing love. They express warmth and compassion to the people whom they have close ties with. The best part is that this is genuine compassion. Psychic empaths cannot possibly fake their love.

Sleep issues

Psychic empaths battle an array of sleep-related problems. Their sleep problems probably began in early childhood. The issues may range from bed-wetting, nightmares, and even insomnia. Of course, these sleep-related issues have had a negative effect on their quality of life.

Good at connecting dots

Psychic empaths are extremely creative, and they can piece together disjointed parts to form a whole. Their ability to connect dots enables them to find solutions to existential problems. If they develop their creative potential, they can end up becoming innovators or great artists. Many psychic empaths tend to obsess about connecting these dots so that when one piece is complete, they quickly start connecting the next set of dots.

They have trouble letting go

Psychic empaths don't open their hearts at everyone trying to catch their interest. However, once they open their hearts, they tend to love with a ferocious will. For this reason, terminating a relationship with a psychic empath would be disastrous. They have trouble letting go after investing much of their emotions into the relationship.

Chapter 27: The Difference Between Empaths and Highly Sensitive People

Though highly sensitive people and empaths almost seem to read from the same script, there are actually some differences between the two. What you must first understand is that being a highly sensitive person or an empath is not mutually exclusive. You can be both of them at the same time. The following are some differences between highly sensitive people and empaths:

Highly sensitive people take longer to wind down and restore their energy than empaths

Both empaths and highly sensitive people tend to get overstimulated after spending the day mixing with other people. While empaths recover from the overstimulation much quicker, highly sensitive people need much more time to recover from the overstimulation. For this reason, a highly sensitive person will seclude themselves much longer than the empath. Highly sensitive people, as the name suggests, tend to dwell too much on their sensory experiences. Their brains are wired in such peculiar ways to listen for certain keywords.

A highly sensitive person usually has a number of insecurities that make them incredibly self-conscious. It doesn't matter how perfect they seem to the average person, but once this insecurity creeps up on the said person, then it can be quite hard to overcome the insecurity. For instance, if someone grew up feeling ugly, they might internalize this feeling to the extent that no one will help them see themselves in a different light. When that person goes out and realizes people are giving them stares, they will automatically think that people are analyzing their looks and finding them ugly.

This will set off the alarm in their head about how ugly they are and what follows is a streak of obsessive thoughts. When a person is extremely sensitive, they tend to be sensitive about virtually everything. When they move from one concern, they will immediately find something else to stress about. On the other hand, empaths are sensitive, yes, but they are sensitive to the energies floating around them. This means that they stop feeling terrible once the source of their distress moves away from them. For this reason, after a day of mingling with people, empaths are in a far much better position to restore their energy than highly sensitive people.

Highly sensitive people are introverts whereas empaths can be either introverts or extroverts

For both highly sensitive people and empaths, the commonest personality spectrum that they share is that of introversion. Highly sensitive people are exclusively introverts whereas empaths – though a majority of them are introverts – could just as well be extroverted. To understand why a highly sensitive person has no chance of ever being an extrovert, you have to understand how their mind works. A highly sensitive person has beliefs in their mind that they keep looking for supporting evidence. Due to their extremely sensitive nature, they keep misreading what people meant. For instance, if a lecturer attends a session and keeps focusing his gaze on a certain highly sensitive girl, the girl might think that something is wrong with them, but unbeknownst to them, the lecturer actually finds them attractive to look at.

So, the girl will obsess about everything they think is wrong with them and this cycle of thought is absolutely draining. Ultimately, they will have to retire into some quiet place to regain their composure and energy. They cannot do without having to retreat into their caves – the classic introvert tendency. On the other hand, an empath plays the role of an emotional sponge. They tend to pick up on the vibrations of the people around them. If they are around good people, they feel good, and if they are around bad people, they start feeling bad themselves. This can also drive them to seek solitude. Except that there are empowered empaths who understand the condition that they struggle with.

An extroverted empath will choose to stay away from people who prey on their energy and associate with the good-natured ones instead. In other words, an extroverted empath will take advantage of their ability to soak up people's energies by choosing to soak up the positive energy.

Empaths can sense the subtlest energy

The ability of the highly sensitive people to pick up on subtle energies is not as fine-tuned as that of empaths. An empath can detect even the tiniest bit of emotion because they are connected to people on a very primal level. The empath seems to be able to access a person's mind and gain total access to their emotions. On the other hand, though a highly sensitive person would pick up on the energy of other people, they will merely pick up the general vibe and miss out on the subtlety. An empath is much more likely to go through the rollercoaster of emotions, but a highly sensitive person is stuck in a cycle of negative thoughts once triggered.

Empaths internalize the feelings of other people

When an empath perceives the emotions of other people, it doesn't stop there. They upgrade other people's emotions to become their own. Thus, if someone is in a world of pain, the empath is forced to feel the pain too. In that sense, the empath is at the mercy of the people that they interact with.

Highly sensitive people cannot internalize the feelings of other people. They have a million insecurities – real and imagined. What happens is that someone will say something or do something and the highly sensitive person will be triggered. Highly sensitive people have very sharp observation skills, and they vet people's deeds against their database of insecurities. Once the negative train of thoughts starts, there's no stopping.

Empaths have trouble distinguishing someone else's discomfort as their own

As an empath, you could be sitting in a lecture hall, trying to pay attention, and then *bam!* You start experiencing agonizing thoughts. Even though you have internalized those thoughts, you cannot tell the source. So, you just suffer quietly. On the other hand, the highly sensitive person can tell apart their emotional distress from those of others.

Chapter 28: How to Boost Your Psychic Abilities

Although you have psychic potential, you still have to train yourself so that your skills may become finely tuned. The following are some tips to help you enhance your psychic abilities:

Meditate everyday

Meditation allows you to raise your vibration. The spirit energy vibrates at a high frequency. Through meditation, you can heighten your mental and spiritual powers and become capable of performing even greater psychic acts. Meditation is not a resource-intensive activity. You can pull it off almost anywhere. You just require a serene environment and some free time.

Communicate with your spirit guide

Your spirit guide is basically an entity that protects you. They also enlighten you and make you insightful. When you call on their support, you will increase your chances of achieving what you desire. Have a sacred place in which you meet your spirit guide.

Use psychometry

Psychometry is the practice of decoding the energies of an object. If you can become skilled in this discipline, you will receive a tremendous boost to your psychic abilities. Acquire an object that has sentimental value – e.g., a wedding band – and try to envision the energies of the owner.

Flower visualization

To have strong psychic abilities, you have to improve your mind's eye. You can achieve this through flower visualization. The exercise entails picking up a few flowers and holding them in front of you. Now close your eyes and start envisioning each of them separately.

Random visualization

When you are done using the flower to strengthen your mind's eye, you may now explore some randomness. Just close your eyes and lie on your back in a serene environment and invite your spirit guides to show you many great wonders of the universe. Your spirit guides should show you magnificent images and videos.

Take a walk in nature

Psychics feel a tremendous connection with nature. You could take a stroll in a nature park while practicing mindful meditation. Take occasional stops by sweet-smelling flowers and savor their beauty. Lose yourself to the beauty of nature.

Eliminate negativity

You cannot tap into your psychic powers if you harbor tons of negativity. Eliminate your negativity by heightening your self-awareness and being more forgiving to yourself. You also have to take the necessary steps to right the wrongs you have done. Once you're free of negativity, you're in the right headspace to employ your psychic powers.

Believe in yourself

You cannot become a skilled clairvoyant unless you have tremendous belief in yourself. One of the ways of increasing your self-belief is through reading about those before you who have succeeded. Find books written by successful clairvoyants and read about them so that you can become familiar with their stories. Learn their tricks. The more you study about successful clairvoyants, the higher your odds of becoming successful yourself.

Rest

Quality rest is absolutely necessary. The more you rest, the more energy you have to channel into your psychic activities. One of the best ways to ensure quality rest is by getting enough sleep. You should get at least six hours of sleep every night. This will ensure that your mind is well rested and you're in top physical condition. Having enough rest is crucial for the development of your clairvoyant skills.

Try to read other people's thoughts

This is a perfect way of strengthening your clairvoyant abilities. When you encounter someone, just gaze into their eyes and try to imagine what they are thinking about. If you can accurately read people's minds, then you can rest assured that your psychic abilities are very well developed.

Keep track of your dreams

People with psychic abilities tend to dream a lot. After each dream, ensure you have noted it down on a journal. This will help you keep track of the dreams that came true. When you realize that your dreams are starting to become true, it indicates that your clairvoyant abilities are getting fine-tuned.

Improve your remote-viewing capability

Remote-viewing is the ability to view a place or an event through your mind's eye without you being physically present. To improve your ability of remote-viewing, you have to make good use of your imagination. Start with viewing places near you, and when you get them right, you can move on to far-flung places and objects.

Overcome your fears

If you have any fear in your mind, you will not achieve your full potential as a clairvoyant. You have to eliminate the fear to be able to channel all your mental energies in your psychic activities. The first step toward eliminating fear is to increase your knowledge. The more you know about a situation, the less ignorant you are and the more power and courage you acquire.

Resolve your differences with those around you

If you have problems with other people, ensure that you resolve them. You cannot achieve your full clairvoyant potential when you are not at peace with yourself or other people. Cast away the burden of bitterness and resolve your differences with those around you. This way, your mind is in a position to channel its energies into psychic activities.

Practice seeing auras

This is another great exercise for improving your psychic abilities. Have your friend stand next to a plain-colored wall. Then, look at them using your third eye. Notice if you get to see their auric field. If they have a high vibration, their aura will appear bright.

Ask a friend to call you

Contact your friend telepathically and ask them to give you a call. The more mental energy you invest in this activity, the more likely your friend will call you.

If an empath developed their psychic potential, they could end up becoming so skilled that a career along that line would be in order.

Conclusion

An empath is a person with the special gift of picking up on the energies of the people around them and believing them to be their own. These are the categories of empaths:

- **Emotion empaths**: They pick up on the emotions of other people and believe them to be their own. If they stay near sad people, they end up becoming sad, and if they stay near happy people, they end up feeling happy.
- **Medical empaths**: They can detect the physical status of other people's bodies. They can tell what's ailing a particular person in an instant.
- **Geomantic empaths**: They are attuned to certain environments or landscapes.
- **Plant empaths**: They share a connection with plant life. They can intuitively communicate with various plants.
- **Animal empaths**: They share a strong connection with animals. Animals trust them, and they can sense their feelings.
- **Intuitive empaths**: They can pick up information from people by paying heed to their gut feeling.

- **Psychometric empaths**: They can pick up the energy from various objects.
- **Precognitive empaths**: They are aware of future events long before they take place.

Check out another book by Steven Turner

Made in the USA
Las Vegas, NV
24 March 2024

87706796R00075